LADY PENELOPE

The pen name Lady Penelope is chosen because she was regarded as one of the most considerate and polite people of her time. When her husband Ulysses failed to return from the wars she was beseiged by suitors, who assumed that her man had been killed.

One after another these men proposed marriage but being an astute woman of impeccable loyalty, instead of refusing them, she explained "I will not decide whom I shall marry until I finish knitting this jersey" (she had started it to have it ready for her husband on his return).

As the months passed to years the jersey grew longer and longer but this diplomatic ruse enabled Penelope to hold off her suitors, while remaining courteous to them all and loyal to her husband.

In the same series:

Wedding Etiquette Properly Explained
Best Man's Duties
Babies Names A–Z
The Select-A-Joke Book
Right Joke For The Right Occasion
Joke After Joke
Sample Social Speeches
General & Social Letter Writing
Write Your Own Will
Right Way To Prove A Will
Divorce

ETIQUETTE TODAY

BY

LADY PENELOPE

PAPERFRONTS
ELLIOT RIGHT WAY BOOKS,
KINGSWOOD, SURREY, U.K.

Made and printed in Great Britain by Robert Hartnoll (1985) Ltd, Bodmin, Cornwall.

CONTENTS

INTRODUCTION

THE UNWRITTEN RULES

We are all, even the most rebellious among us, bound by rules. Some are fixed and rigid, like the laws of the land, others unwritten and implicit and obeyed voluntarily because obedience to them confers valued status. Knowledge of etiquette often helps a career. Most of us belong to groups of one sort or another, among which, once we are accepted, we feel at ease. Equally, most of us sometimes find ourselves in situations where we flounder because we do not know what is expected of us. Some knowledge of manners enables us to fade into the scenery and not attract undue attention to ourselves, to take our place in events happily and enjoy them fully.

In the Swinging Sixties it became fashionable to flout long-standing conventions and many hitherto exclusive institutions were invaded by people who had previously been unacceptable outsiders. This minor revolution brought insecurity and unease with it and it is noticeable that, for instance, now we are encouraged to express our personalities in our dress at all times, it is even more possible to feel wrongly attired at a social gathering than when we were told exactly what to wear. There is infinitely greater choice in dress for most than a generation ago but it is still helpful to know, for instance, that "white tie" on an invitation (rarely used now) indicates full evening dress for women, "black tie" a cocktail dress and "lounge suit" something considerably less formal. Women take their cue from and must follow the instruction for men.

It is said the British are a class-ridden society. That has some truth. Our society has evolved over centuries and it is not possible to throw away what has become part of the structure of the way we live. There is a security in knowing your roots and where you belong. However, our society offers boundless opportunities to scale the barriers of class and custom and this book is written for those who wish to augment their own good sense with a knowledge of what is expected of them, in what may be unfamiliar surroundings. It is hoped they will acquire confidence which owes nothing to arrogance or affectation but much to being valued members of the circles in which they move. Good taste and behaviour have grown out of the Christian teaching that we do to others as we would like them to do to us. "The essence", it is said, "of good manners, is thoughtfulness for others". This is a scarce asset today and the words "he's a gentleman" may apply with equal truth to a jobbing gardener or a sovereign.

ACKNOWLEDGEMENTS

I would like to thank a surgeon friend and several experts in their own fields of cooking, hunting and cricket and I am most grateful for their time and help.

In writing a book like this the author has to cull her ideas from far and wide and therefore I would like to acknowledge with gratitude several go-ahead newspapers such as The Daily Telegraph, the Daily Mail, Daily Express, and Daily Mirror as well as great magazines such as Woman's Own, Woman, Woman's Weekly and She. Stonemans of Reigate very kindly gave me some guidance on the subject of funerals.

To my secretary for her endless patience and guidance and to anyone whom I may have overlooked I say "thank you", but in the words of the great American President, Harry Truman, "the buck stops here", therefore if there are any errors the fault is mine.

1

ON ENTERTAINING

Most of us find it necessary to offer hospitality sooner or later. There are a few souls who appear never to usher friends over their threshold; perhaps they dish out hospitality on neutral ground somewhere (pub or club?) in order to cut down the homework but I think it safe to say that where the welcome is thin the mantelpiece will hardly be sagging under the weight of received invitations! Entertaining should not be a burden; you need follow no standards but your own. Your guests will be comfortable when you are comfortable so choose the date and time to suit yourself. Invite your guests in such a way that your intentions are clear, put your best into your preparations then relax and enjoy their company. Many invitations are given by word of mouth, sometimes on the spur of the moment. Where you are on less free-and-easy terms with your intended guests it is better to send a written invitation, giving date, time and, where advisable, some idea when you expect them to leave. An advantage of a written invitation is that it is less likely to be forgotten, e.g.

> Dear Mrs. Smith, (or "Joan" if you are on Christian name terms),
>   John/my husband and I will be delighted if you and your husband/Bill can come for lunch here on Sunday, June 16th at 12.30 p.m. We will hope for a fine day and try to tempt you to a relaxed country walk before you return to town.
> > With greetings,
> > > Signature,

(NB Chapter 13 details various forms of invitation as a guide for different occasions.)

TIME TO GO
Many a promising friendship has floundered on the rocks of "outstaying one's welcome". There are conventional times for

offering hospitality – coffee time, lunch, dinner, supper or tea, cocktail time or even coffee in the evening. A few items such as crisps, nuts, biscuits or cake, sweets, etc., are usually offered with coffee, tea or drinks.

PARTY TIMES

Morning coffee is usually from 10.30 a.m. or 11.00 a.m. and you should give your guests the choice of black or white. Serve it in a jug or a percolator, pour it black and offer cream or milk, together with sugar in a bowl. Some say that hot milk ruins coffee; it is a matter of taste but you can't go wrong if you serve thin cream, which is always served cold. Others believe that brown sugar alters the flavour too much and prefer white sugar – perhaps both should be available. A dish of biscuits, or a light cake help to reduce the gap between breakfast and lunch but your guests may decline food for many people are figure-conscious, preferring not to be embarrassed by any over-insistent offer of food.

If your guests have arrived at 10.30 a.m. and show no sign of leaving by noon – and you feel it is time for them to go – you can suggest they do so gracefully by standing up at a suitable pause in the conversation and offering them a glass of sherry, without being too pressing (keep a bottle of medium/dry sherry handy). They normally ought to leave by 12.30. If they linger, think of something that requires your presence elsewhere or work out some other courteous reason – people who outstay their welcome are a nuisance.

Lunch invitations are for any time after twelve (it's best to specify the time); don't ask guests early if you know you will be in a last minute panic getting redder and redder over the hot stove and, for heaven's sake, don't be too ambitious about the menu. You should always be ready for your guests so that you can give them your entire attention and make them feel at home – even those who arrive early, although in my book it is as rude and inconsiderate to arrive too soon as too late. Do what comes easily to you and save elaborate menus for when you have time to perfect them.

WELCOME YOUR GUESTS

If you are giving a big party you will need someone at the door to take coats and show guests the cloakroom – best to have one room where the ladies can tidy-up after a journey. Be sure all guests know where the lavatory is as shy folk may not care to ask.

On welcoming your guests it is usual to offer them a drink. No need to set up a bar in your sitting-room. You can provide a choice of sherries – dry and medium, perhaps beer or lager (chilled) and chilled fresh orange-juice, which is good by itself and equally good diluted with tonic or soda water. It is not necessary to lay in bottles of gin and whisky if you are not accustomed to using these and many people keep their consumption of alcohol during the daytime to a minimum. Plain tonic water, chilled with a slice of lemon, is very refreshing before lunch or at any time.

Half-an-hour is enough for these preliminaries and allows time to re-fill or top up your guest's glasses.

FLOWERS

Flowers on the table and in the house help to "lift" the atmosphere and, provide a subject for conversation if the going is sticky. *Exclusively* red and white flowers at table are considered by some people to be unlucky.

VARIOUS DISHES

Lunch dishes can be simple and no starter course is required unless you wish. If you are entertaining without help in the kitchen, it makes sense to serve something that is complete in itself and can be heated in the oven while you enjoy a drink with your guests – it is important that you should be with them and not dashing in and out as this imparts a sense of unease!

Savoury dishes, such as macaroni cheese, lasagne, fish pie and fish cheese are first-class for lunch, as are shepherd's pie and sausage pie or any casseroled dish that includes vegetables with the meat. Fresh bread rolls can be popped into the hot oven while you dish up the rest of the food; bread is a satisfying addition to a meal and is improved by a *short* stay in a hot oven.

Pudding should balance your main course; if you have served fish/cheese, for instance, some sort of fruit pie with cream will not be too heavy. If you have produced something substantial first then pudding should be light – a cold lemon soufflé perhaps, fresh fruit or that perennial favourite with almost everyone, chocolate mousse. None of these are difficult and the recipes can be found in any good cookery-book, but even simpler is good ice-cream with chocolate or fruit sauce or the nicest yoghurt you can find. Try mixing equal quantities of plain yoghurt and whipped double cream, pouring it over frozen, fresh or canned (and strained) raspberries in an attractive dish, spreading a thick layer of soft brown sugar over the top and putting the whole thing in the fridge for two or three hours.

Offer cheese and biscuits after this if your budget runs to it, or give it as an alternative. It isn't necessary to offer second helpings; if you don't you may have enough left for supper!

COFFEE AND AFTER

Coffee can be taken at the table, but if you decide to serve it in your drawing room that makes an opportunity for your guests to be offered the cloakroom (where they should find fresh towels and paper tissues as well as a decent piece of soap). If you have a separate dining room, you should shut the door after the meal. Following coffee and a reasonable interval your guests should be thinking of going: unless you are having a rollicking time which it would be a pity to break up. If, however, you've had enough try rising and murmuring about fetching more coffee – you'll never "win" from a sitting position!

Remember to offer use of the bathroom before friends leave.

HIGH TEAS AND TEAS

In the context of entertaining "tea" usually means afternoon tea at four o'clock, or thereabouts, and not the meal referred to as tea (more correctly "high" tea) which is the early evening meal enjoyed by a large number of Britons. This latter can be a sumptuous meal and if invited to one you might expect to be offered fish or bacon and egg or an egg dish followed by a selection of teabreads, scones, pancakes, oatcakes, etc., with jam, or honey, and perhaps a slice of homemade cake all washed down by lashings of hot tea.

If you are planning the four o'clock afternoon tea, good presentation inexplicably adds to the flavour. Get out your best china, iron your prettiest tablecloth and find some small napkins – no reason why they should not be the better sort of soft crumbly paper ones to save work. Knock up some sandwiches of thin bread and butter and cucumber (thinly sliced with peel left on to prevent indigestion) or cut a plateful of thin bread and butter and offer either your own home-made jam or the best shop jam you can afford. If you want decant the jam into a pretty dish, but a good, honest jam jar standing on a clean saucer is an acceptable vessel. Give it a clean spoon.

One need not provide more than one cake – some people find fruit cake with tea an indigestible mixture and some can't bear sponges – so, if you want to be sure of catering to everyone's taste, provide a variety of, say, a Madeira cake, a gingerbread and some shortbread with your sandwiches or bread (or scones or dropscones), butter and jam. Children will polish off all left-overs when they get home or they can be used up in packed lunches. You can prepare sandwiches in the morning and wrap them in a cloth wrung out in water to keep them moist if your time is precious, until just before guests arrive. Tea is usually consumed in the dining room but there is nothing cosier than tea beside the drawing room fire in the winter.

People used to have special dishes in which buttered toast or crumpets could be kept hot by the fire; and real lace doilies were used on cake-plates. Paper doilies are easily obtained from stationers, but they are less essential today, and ordinary napkins are used.

DRINKS SERVED AT PARTIES

If you are planning to have a drinks party or to invite a few friends to a quiet drink, around six-thirty is the time (later in some large cities except at weekends) so that it can be enjoyed as a prelude to dinner. This gives you time before your guests leave for their evening meal and thank you for your hospitality. The drinks you offer depend on what you can afford – which may depend on the number of guests.

Spirits are costly as are the "eats" that go with them and you will be surprised how the average drinker's capacity for strong drink alters according to whether or not he is paying for the stuff! Be honest with yourself and your guests and don't offer them "whatever you like" if your range consists of a bottle of inferior sherry, the dregs of a bottle of red wine and some sloe gin bought at the last Christmas Fayre. Equally, unless you are an expert, home-made wine that started life as a mush in a bucket in your kitchen isn't likely to go down too well; I once was impelled to offer rather cloudy home-made wine to some visitors who turned up unexpectedly at the awkward hour after tea and before drinks time; one of them turned out to be a member of the Vintners' Company. I still like his wife.

Stronger Drinks

If you can afford it offer gin and whisky, with tonic water and bitter lemon for the gin and soda water and a jug of plain water (or Malvern water or Perrier) for the whisky. A bottle of dry sherry and one of medium sherry, some fresh, chilled orange juice and some ice and lemon slices will give your guests a good choice. Provide some nuts (dry roasted peanuts are good and popular) and the health food shops and better supermarkets can provide all sorts of tasty things to nibble. If you don't want to lash out on spirits, buy a bottle or two (if it is a small party) of the best all-purpose (medium) sherry you can afford or serve red or white wine, the white well chilled and the red left, cork drawn, at room temperature for an hour or two especially if the wine was cold.

Borrow Glasses If Need

Your local wine merchant will advise on what to get and should lend you glasses if you need them; different drinks require differently shaped glasses (no tooth mugs please) but off-licences stock useful all-purpose glasses for wine and soft drinks. Whisky should be served in a nice tumbler.

From the left: Cocktail, sherry, wine, brandy balloon, whisky, champagne, liqueur.

DRINKS AND EATS

Drinks parties at which "finger food" is served can begin later at 7.00 or 7.30 p.m. – because if your guests tuck in to your delicious food with enthusiasm they won't want a meal as well. Here again, you can have a supply of most drinks or serve wine. If you're pushing the boat out, champagne cocktails first, later topped up with champagne. Trays of vol-au-vents filled with chicken in sauce or fish, savoury things on fried bread (doesn't go soggy like toast or biscuits) asparagus rolls, hot cocktail sausages, smoked salmon sandwiches, choux pastry buns filled with savoury mixtures and cubes of cheese on "sticks" with tiny onions and pieces of tinned pineapple all serve as good blotting paper!

HELPERS

At all good parties, except the smallest, it is essential to detail one or more friends to pass the trays of eats round regularly, until everyone has had enough. Children love doing this but they need to be supervised to make sure they don't pester people, or forget to go round a sufficient number of times. At large parties several people may be required to help as some people don't like to go to the tables to help themselves.

Passing drink round is an adult job. Everyone at the start of any party ought to be provided with a drink but it is vital to offer to replenish glasses as they become empty.

A WARNING

Please don't pester guests to refill their glasses. Offer yes, but never press as doing so is treble-edged.

a)   It can be embarrassing to refuse.
b)   It can keep police busy after the party!
c)   It adds greatly to the cost!

It is no longer usual to provide cigarettes as smoking has come to be regarded by many as anti-social but ash trays are essential.

Courtesy and consideration for friends are an important part of etiquette, as of all life; indeed, if you were to conduct all your affairs with regard to other people's comfort, convenience and happiness, and if everyone did the same there would be no need for rules of etiquette. As the world becomes more of a jungle we can but continue to pioneer in being good neighbours. If you are planning a party that may disturb neighbours warn them so that they can arrange to go out or disarm them with an invitation.

THE SUCCESSFUL DINNER

There may come a time when you feel you want – or ought – to give a dinner-party, rather than asking people round for supper. It is a pleasant way of offering hospitality to friends or business associates. Operate within your capabilities and allow time to prepare. You don't have to spring-clean the house first, but be sure it is tidy and welcoming with no heaps of newspapers in the corners or dead daffodils in vases. Strangers don't usually notice details like cushions coming unstitched or rugs askew so ignore them yourself and relax once your guests have arrived.

There are several vital ingredients in a successful dinner-party; the food and drink are important, your house should be warm and welcoming (or in Summer cool and welcoming!) and, if possible, be filled with flowers while the host and hostess should be in command of themselves, their family, pets and for the time being, their guests.

VITAL TO GET RIGHT MIX OF GUESTS

There is one prime ingredient without which your party may collapse like a cake without a raising-agent. It is this; the mixture of guests should be carefully thought out to ensure that there are some links between them of shared experience, interest or some bond that they should take delight in discovering. Select your guests with skill and you will be amazed how your party will take off. Plan the meal sensibly, balancing the courses, if you mean to have more than two, so that you get variety of textures, flavours and content. Choose a main course that can be prepared and then left in the oven or a heated trolley (very useful, these) and don't for goodness sake, opt for something that has to be deep-fried, unless you have a kitchen several smell-proof miles away. Nothing clings like the smell of hot fat or permeates a house so quickly and you run the risk of re-joining your guests, as I did once, with globules of fat on your skirt. It is usual to serve three or four courses at a dinner – an entree, or starter, which can be soup, a savoury soufflé, fish in a savoury sauce (cold or hot) or – that standby, pâté with freshly-made toast. None of these should be served in such quantity that your guests' appetites are dulled before the main course. The starter should tickle the palate, not suffocate it. Serve it attractively on pretty china.

VARIOUS COURSES

The main course can be a roast or something in a casserole or in a sauce and there is a wide range of meats to choose from if you or your guests are not vegetarian. You will, of course serve vegetables, with rice or noodles sometimes taking the place of potatoes. A green salad is often liked and requires an extra small plate placed in front of each guest above the dinner plate.

CARVING

Food that has been carefully cooked deserves to be well presented. To carve well in front of your guests is spectacular and satisfying. If you are nervous your wife may carve or some dishes may be served in the kitchen and reformed to give appetising results.

Although boned and rolled joints are very popular, joints cooked on the bone tend to be more succulent and lose less weight due to shrinkage.

The basic requirements are a stiff bladed carving knife, a large fork and a carving board. To keep the knife sharp a butcher's steel is perhaps the best. Hold the steel firmly in one hand and run the blade of the knife away from you up the shaft at a narrow angle, then repeat on the other side of the blade. A butcher sharpens towards his hand, but pointing the blade outwards is as effective and safe. If a steel is not available use a carborundum stone or one of the knife sharpeners that can be bought. A sharp knife is safer and easier to use.

Beef

Roast rib of beef is also a traditional Sunday lunch. When buying a rib joint ask your butcher to saw through the backbone to make the final carving easier. After roasting, all meats are easier to carve if allowed to rest for a few minutes in a warm place. First if possible remove the backbone, so that the knife can easily cut down to the rib

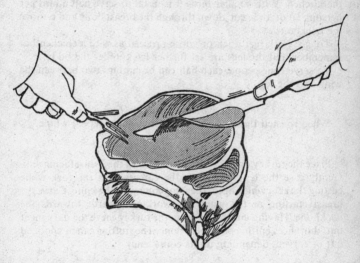

RIB OF BEEF: Shows how this is cut. Should anyone carve towards their hand make sure that the safety prong of the fork is up (as shown).

bones. When the knife reaches the bone ease the slice of meat off the bone, onto the plate. Use the whole length of the knife's blade as if it were a saw. The sharpness of the blade will do the work with little downward pressure. Rolled joints, sirloin and fillet should also be carved across the grain of the meat with the same back and forward knife action. The slices of meat should be approximately $\frac{1}{4}$ inch thick.

Chicken, Pheasant, etc.

Lift the chicken by placing the carving fork inside the bird and drain before placing on the carving board. Lay the chicken on its back and with the fork in its breast, cut the skin between the carcass and the leg and ease the leg and drum-stick away with the knife. Repeat with the other leg. Having removed the legs, cut them in half between the thigh and the drumstick. Cut through the breast directly above the wing joints and remove both wings, then carve the remainder of the breast.

Duck and Goose

Carving duck and goose can be messy so it is perhaps best done in the kitchen. With smaller birds it is usual to serve half a bird per person. To do this, cut down through the breast bone and remove the backbone.

To carve a larger duck or goose proceed as with a chicken but remember that the legs are set further back under the body.

To serve four people each half can be cut into two between the wing and the leg.

Pigeon, Partridge, Grouse, Etc.

When roasted these smaller birds are usually served whole.

Turkey

Place the turkey on the carving board with the breast facing you. Gently ease the leg away from the carcass with the fork while cutting the skin which holds them together with the knife. Carve the breast starting at the wing and working inwards towards the backbone. Having cut the leg from the turkey carve the dark meat into thin slices cutting parallel to bone. The stuffing can be spooned out or carved, depending on its consistency.

Lamb – Leg

Allow to rest in a warm place for a few minutes, then place on the carving dish with the narrow bone towards you and with the more rounded side uppermost. With the carving fork securely in the small knuckle of meat nearest to you, carve a wedge out of the leg near to the fork. Now carve towards you carving slices of lamb at an angle of 45°, making sure you cut right to the bone on each slice. As the slices become thicker turn the leg from side to side. Now turn the leg over and carve the remaining meat parallel to the bone.

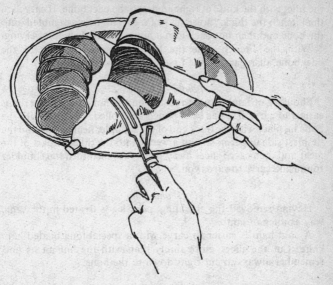

Carving a leg of lamb into nice pieces.

Lamb – Saddle

There are two ways of carving the saddle, the English and the French method. With the English method a cut is made down each side of the backbone, then the meat is carved at a slight slant across

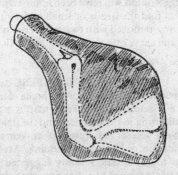

Shows the bone in a right hand shoulder of lamb.

the fillet with the knife at right angles to the backbone. If carved in the kitchen the thick "noisettes" of meat can be reassembled onto the bone and then put back into a hot oven briefly before serving.

With the French style the lamb is carved parallel to the backbone, disregarding the first slice as it will be all fat.

Lamb – Shoulder

Shoulder of lamb can be roasted on the bone but it is perhaps easiest to carve if it has been boned and rolled. To carve with the bone in, place with the thick end of the shoulder nearest you and the fleshiest side uppermost. Cut a wedge into the thickest part of the meat and then carve slices away from you, then turn the shoulder round and carve towards you.

Pork and Ham

Having removed the crackling, pork leg is treated in the same way as a leg of lamb.

A cold ham is easier to carve with a special long bladed ham knife. Cut the slices more thinly than with the hot meats and remember always to cut right down to the bone.

Saddle of Hare

The meat from the cooked saddle of hare should come away easily from the bone. Ease the two fillets away from the backbone with a small strong knife and slice into small rounds if required.

Side of Smoked Salmon

Place the salmon skin down parallel to the edge of the table. The main bones of the salmon will have been removed prior to smoking but you may still find the heads of small bones running down its flank. These can be removed with tweezers. Trim off any flesh that is hard or dark and carve into very thin slices at a flat angle towards the tail.

PUDDINGS AND CHEESE

Now comes pudding, although some who have travelled abroad like to produce a selection of cheeses at this point. The more conventional still bring in the pud here and the field is wide. Don't make it apple pie if you served prawn vol-au-vents as a starter but don't despise the plain, old fashioned puddings. My husband, never an innovator in food matters, recently suggested that we should serve steamed treacle sponge at a dinner party – we did and it was acclaimed! After this produce cheese or something cheesy; half of your guests may decline, feeling satisfied. Those who accept will probably want a cheese biscuit; be sure the biscuits are crisp and not bendy. And throughout the meal have wholesome bread, rolls, breadsticks, Melba toast or Ryvita with butter available in an attractive dish.

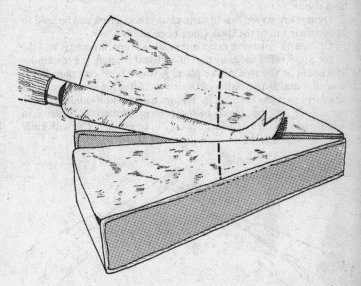

THE RIGHT WAY TO CUT CHEESE. The dotted line shows how it should *not* be done because the tip would normally be the most mature section. The method shown divides fairly for all.

EATING PROBLEMS

Pâté is an item which may seem a little frightening to the un-initiated. This arrives on a plate and you help yourself or is served individually. It can be eaten with a fork but often with fingers of toast or bread onto which a mouthful of the pâté is trowelled.

Caviare is served ice cold often with a taste of lemon. It may come in a bowl or on a plate from which each guest spoons a small quantity onto his plate. Fresh toast fingers are available which act as a trowel to shovel up a few morsels of this delicacy. It is an acquired taste, not favoured by everyone. It is sometimes served in individual dishes as a starter, with a creamy mayonnaise on top eaten with a teaspoon.

Supping soup; push the spoon away from you to the far side of the bowl, in order to fill it. Oddly, failure to do this is seen as a sign of ignorance. A silly rule which survives.

Mussels are served cooked and with a sauce, eaten with a fork and spoon.

Oysters are served raw in various ways and a fork can be used to scoop them out of the shell. Chew once and swallow.

Globe artichokes are eaten one petal at a time, dipping it into the sauce provided. The fleshy part of each leaf is eaten, the remainder discarded to the side of the plate. A finger bowl (see page 25) is essential during the eating of the leaves. After the leaves are off, if the furry part has been left in, remove it with a knife and fork. The remainder of the heart below (except perhaps a little skin underneath) is now a further delicacy to be relished. Cut with knife and eat with a fork.

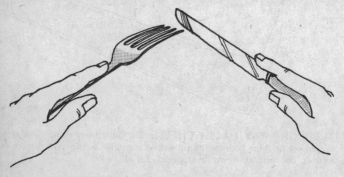

HOLDING A KNIFE AND FORK CORRECTLY. A common error is to hold the knife as if it were a pencil or a hammer. Not done!

Tricky Pea Problem

Put some mashed potato on the fork and then using your knife press the peas into the mash. Another way is to reverse the fork and load the peas onto the prongs but you need a steady hand. Shaky people could refuse the pea course! The difficulty of using a spoon for the peas or gravy is less a matter of etiquette than that you tend to run out of spoons! All I can say is do not pick the peas up with your fingers or try to eat them off the knife! There is room for initiative in pea eating.

Removing Bones or Pips

Years ago a fuss was made over this. One had to push the intruder with one's tongue onto one's fork or spoon but there is little against picking it out with the fingers except that it makes them sticky. Lay the pip on the edge of your plate. If a pip or bone gets under your artificial teeth ask to go to the cloakroom rather than suffer.

Grapes present a problem of pips which correctly should be pushed out with the tongue on to a fork but in practice can be removed between thumb and finger. Never pick single grapes from the bowl. Cut yourself a small cluster, then pick.

Finger Eating

It is done to hold your corn on the cob and bite the grains off. Folk with teeth problems may have to use a knife and fork, and

FINGER BOWLS: These are rare but at a few functions you will find one at each place setting. I mention them because on my first encounter with one, I took a drink out of it! Alternatively, they are brought round on a tray for the guests. A napkin is used to dry the fingers.

scrape the corn off the cob. Where the cob is skewered it is easier.

If finger bowls are provided dip fingers in and dry off with a serviette, but a serviette alone may be enough.

Other foods eaten by hand include asparagus, sometimes served in a vase-type dish, artichokes and celery often accompanying or following the meat course.

Fruit Knives and Eating Fruit

At some functions fruit is eaten with a fruit knife and fork for example where one might skin and eat an apple or peach but customs change and most top people use their hands in the ordinary way. A finger bowl has a use, particularly at dinner dances where one may be caressing one's partner's clothing.

NOT WORTH A THOUGHT

Worrying as these matters appear to the inexperienced fear not because you can always watch and follow somebody else when in any etiquette doubt – unless they are slouching with their elbows on the table – this can only be done with old friends. Nor should you be shy to enquire of a neighbour or friend if a problem arises. In the next section we mention the setting of the table for knives and forks, etc., and below we give an illustration of a number of items of cutlery set for table. Meals of over four courses are unusual. We reiterate that one usually starts with the implements at the outside and "work" inwards.

HOW TO SET THE TABLE

Many people are worried and confused by table setting. It isn't really complicated and, like all rules of etiquette, the rules are meant to be helpful and to put you at your ease. It doesn't matter whether you use a tablecloth or good mats but the placing of the cutlery matters because, *working from the outside inwards*, each course is catered for. The position of cutlery is vital as this is the way your guests can know which implement to use – first course pick up implement(s) at the outside, second course inside that and so on.

For instance, if you start with soup, a soup spoon should be placed at outside right (incidentally, soup should be quietly supped from the *side* of the spoon) and the knife and fork for the main course then take their place next at either side of the place setting. Next in are the fish knife and fork (if needed). The spoon and fork for pudding take their places on the insides or sometimes the pudding or sweet implements are placed across the top.

SETTING A TABLE: We have not shown a side plate or napkin, but if there is a side plate it would be on the left with the napkin. The small knife at the top can be put on the side plate. Even if there is only one choice of wine, there should be two glasses as sometimes another drink or water is required.

The small knife for buttering bread is best put horizontally across the top of the place setting unless there is no soup spoon in which case it can go outside right. If there is a side plate (good if space) the buttering knife can be laid on it. If you are going to serve a savoury or fruit (nice and easy) which require knife and fork these may be brought to the table later with the appropriate plates. For some reason shy guests have been know to panic and become distressed over which tools to use. No need. Millions have used the pudding spoon for the soup.

Napkins

It is best, if you have good linen table napkins, to use them but equally acceptable to use the better quality paper napkins perhaps in a colour which compliments the room, the mats or cloth, and the candles and flowers.

Fish Knives and Forks

In some circles nowadays, fish knives are regarded as a joke. Their use dates back to the days when the gentry had butlers to clean the silver. The smell and taste of fish cling to silver and, in

HOW TO LEAVE YOUR KNIFE AND FORK. The knife and fork are left neatly beside each other; note, one can leave the sharp edge of the knife facing away from the fork (a Scottish custom to save blunting the edge). The soup or pudding spoon is left as shown: if there is also a fork (for the pudding) leave it neatly on the spoon's left. Small but important points.

these days, when most people have to be their own butler, it makes sense either to use all-purpose stainless steel or to keep stainless steel fish knives and forks only for eating fish. (The same, incidentally, applies to egg spoons.) Lack of fish knives and forks should cause no ill reflection on the household.

Wines

If you are serving wine, differently-shaped glasses are traditionally used for red wine and white wine but if your funds don't extend to buying both hock and claret glasses you can hire the all purpose goblet from the off-licence or wine shop which will do quite well. Nor need you worry too much about matching the wine to the meat. It is not essential to offer choice of wine but if you can afford to buy both red and white wine of reasonable quality do so, and be guided by a wine merchant as to which; however be prepared to find that your guests may well prefer to drink white wine with their beef – and, indeed, with everything – and red with their fish and that a delicious hock may please everyone. If you serve fish as a first course, or anything else, for that matter, you can serve sherry with it (not sweet, please).

Do, in any case, remember that some people prefer a soft drink and a jug of iced water on the table is usually welcomed, whether drinking wine or not.

If the meat course doesn't have to be carved it can be handed round unless you have allowed for strictly controlled helpings. In this case you should put the meat on to the plates yourself (preferably at a side table) – pass the choice of vegetables separately – and do make sure there are plenty of them!

Guests should not start eating before the hostess but a good hostess ensures that her guests enjoy hot food by asking them not to wait.

At a dinner or supper party the time to pour out the wine is after the soup but before the meat course. It is not all that important except that one would not pour it at the very start of the meal.

Etiquette (particularly table etiquette) is like the Sabbath, made for man not man for etiquette; thus it is not a thing to lose sleep over. Few people can possibly know all apects of so wide a subject and any minor slips can be smoothed over, if even noticed. We live in a less straight-laced world now but even Queen Victoria was known to pick up turkey bones with her fingers so the beautiful meat next to the bone was not wasted!

MIX THE GUESTS NOT THE DRINKS

When everyone has had enough let the conversation flow for a while but there comes a point where you will want to break up and move away to sit down or to your drawing room. This will ensure that people aren't stuck with each other and you can encourage them to mix around so that no one is left out. This is the time for the ladies to "retire" to the lounge. "Would you like to wash?" is the usual invitation. The men may stay for a while at the dinner-table but, if you take coffee into the sitting room and keep it hot they will soon come to find it. It's all right to remind them if they are too slow! Make sure they also have had the offer of the lavatory.

DEALING WITH DRUNKS

A problem of the car age is what a host is to do if, as will happen at times, a guest gets drunk. One must be iron-willed in trying to prevent him driving home.

Firstly, secure his keys and remove shoes so that he cannot drive away. Secondly, you can try persuading him to drink a few pints of real fruit juice, orange, grapefruit, apple, etc. Coffee, squash and cordials are useless. The real juice helps the liver action. It takes time for this function to work so that ideally the drunkard should sleep for a considerable time until the intoxication clears. Alternatively, someone may be able to take the drunk safely home.

You may require guests to back you up if he is obstreperous but what you want to avoid is him being breathalysed or deaths resulting from an accident. (See also chapter 20.)

2
BEING ENTERTAINED

STAYING WITH OTHERS

Entertaining friends is one thing but being entertained demands different social skills. You are likely to be asked to stay with a number of relatives, school friends, etc., either in your own country or abroad but later you may develop friendships with colleagues at work or friends you have made on holiday or otherwise, who will invite you to stay with them and their hospitality requires that discretion and good manners be your watchwords.

Quite often young people are asked to stay with other young friends during school holidays and it is important for parents to warn their youngsters how to behave. I'm reminded of a young friend aged about 15 who came to stay with us. During my absence he decided to tune-up our lawnmower (which incidentally was not broken) but he managed to break it and this cost me almost half its new price to repair. Guests can be expensive! Children must be told to obey the rules laid down by the host and not to touch things or borrow them, without asking.

PUNCTUALITY

I think there is an old saying "punctuality is the prerogative of kings" but there are not many of them left. When you are asked to visit someone, especially if it is for drinks or a meal, remember the importance of punctuality because to arrive more than a few minutes late shows lack of manners, unless there is a good explanation. To avoid this happening put the name and time on the date in your diary or, if you don't use one, mark your calendar.

Almost equally vital is not to arrive too early. Even five minutes can be upsetting to the hostess who may not quite have got her dress buttoned up, so let the message be watch the time. Few things can upset a party giver like one or more of the guests not arriving – with all the worry as to whether they are coming or not. It must have happened to most of us. You telephone just to make sure that there has not been a muddle over the date and there is no reply so you 'phone again; meanwhile you know that your meal is liable to be spoilt. So please be punctual; ideally the best time to arrive is 5–7 minutes late. Some people think it smart to be 20 to 30 minutes late, but that illustrates their ignorance.

If you are in doubt about the time of the party it is o.k. to enquire but not good manners to 'phone half an hour before, just when the hostess is up to her neck getting ready.

GOING DUTCH

This is an expression which came into use in the late '30s I believe and means that people who are going out together share the cost. Until recently it was the custom for a man taking a woman out to pay for everything but in the last decade or two this has changed. With some girls earning more than their brothers, husbands or boyfriends, naturally if an arrangement can be made, it is fairer for them each to pay their own way. Under the modern women's liberation viewpoint, you might expect some women would *insist* on paying their share but there are no etiquette rules on the matter. In some instances the man will still absorb and prefer to absorb the cost of entertaining the lady. It is wise to discuss the matter freely if in any doubt. That's the modern approach but the more subtle lady "pays back" with a return invitation, by producing theatre tickets or whatever. See also chapter 15.

WHAT TO TAKE WITH YOU (ESPECIALLY FOR SOMEONE IN A NEW HOME)

It is fashionable these days, although it hardly comes under the heading of etiquette, to arrive with a gift especially if the stay is going to be a week or more. For a short overnight visit the choice lies between a gift of beautiful roses for the hostess or a box of confectionery for the family; if it is a longer stay many would bring wine, cheeses, meat, tinned foods, or home-made jams or cakes. One must remember it is very expensive entertaining people in one's home.

Be careful not to embarrass by too much generosity, so use discretion. If the hostess has a garden full of flowers is it not wiser to take chocolates or a bottle of wine? A few bulbs or a small tree or plant for the garden is nice and ideal if going to someone who has moved house. A little fruit tree will be remembered always as your gift. It is considered good luck to take a gift to anyone who has moved to a new home.

THINGS TO AVOID WITH FRIENDS

Your host has gone to much trouble and may have made arrangements to entertain you. He might have planned to watch a cricket match, visit a famous house, or other function and the type of guest who says "I do not want to go" is unlikely to be asked back. Your friend might have organised a party but if you grumble that the room is too hot demanding that windows be opened, you could become a pain in the neck – as well as inducing one. Try to fit in with what is happening and enjoy yourself and avoid any tendency to moan.

DON'T BE A BORE

Occasions arise when you may be landed with the prize village bore; be kind but if he buttonholes you too long, think out an excuse to break away such as "will you excuse me I have got to speak to a friend of mine".

Another problem may be that you find someone in the room whom you don't like. Don't be openly hostile but keep the conversation brief and try and move away as soon as possible.

HELPING OUT

Nowadays people visiting friends generally realise they can help their host or hostess by tidying up their bedroom, making the bed and washing out the bath after use (which a lot of people *forget* to do). So try to leave any room you use including the W.C. the way you found it, clean, and tidy unless you are very good friends and happen to know they are rather Bohemian. I have stayed in homes where practically everything lay on the floor and trying to tidy the place causes consternation! Equally I have stayed with friends who took so much trouble to entertain me that it was more like staying in a Hilton Hotel and although I found this embarrassing one has to fit in and show appreciation.

EVENING THANKS

There are still people, although this may sound a bit "old world" who thank their host and/or hostess each evening of their stay and perhaps kiss goodnight but this would vary according to the station in life and type of people concerned. The new world is badly in need of some old world courtesy, but don't overdo it to embarrass.

Children especially often expect a goodnight cuddle from a guest.

Whatever you do, stick to the rules of the house and avoid what happened to some friends of mine. They had a young visitor in his early 20s and they asked him to be punctual for breakfast at 8.30. He had been called in good time but during his two weeks' stay if he was not half an hour late, he was an hour late. Need I tell you he was never asked back? He thus lost out on some wonderful invitations, because unknown to him, the family he stayed with gave several delightful house parties each year.

MEALS

If you have an allergy and cannot eat fish without your face swelling like a pouter pigeon next morning, then do politely explain before you arrive, by telephone or letter, that you cannot eat fried fish or whatever. Do not say "I cannot eat this", as the fish dish is being served. It is embarrassing but once again we come back to the truth that all etiquette is based on thoughtfulness. If these things are remembered it does not matter whether you are a 14th Earl or plain Mr. Smith.

CLOTHING

The choice of clothing is less important now than it was a generation or two ago. Earlier this century and up to the '40s there were families who dressed in dinner jackets at home every night. There are still families in Britain who dress for evening meals but the "black tie" custom is almost dead.

In town, for a dinner, a darkish lounge suit is more usual while in the country many wear a tweed type suit. Be guided if after a day's golf your hostess remarks "I'm going to change for dinner"; you would follow suit.

Fashion, however, in the matter of dress, alters so rapidly today, that even in good hotels one sees people eating evening meals in country or holiday attire and ours is a free and easy age. Nevertheless there are restaurants and clubs in London and other cities, where one would have to wear a suit or at least a jacket and tie. Jeans would not get past the doorman!

Frequently when visiting friends or functions the room heat builds up and people become uncomfortable. The host or whoever is in charge should pay attention to the ventilation while avoiding draughts. A point of etiquette is whether a man should remove an outer jacket if the room is too hot and the answer is to ask the host if you may. I have often seen this done although one might hesitate at a public function. The host might do so in order to place his guests at liberty to follow (un) suit.

LEAVE EARLY BETTER THAN LATE

As always, there must be no over-staying one's welcome. If you were invited for a week, unless the circumstances are exceptional, do not make it two weeks but remember rules are for fools and wise people use commonsense. So, if you have thoroughly enjoyed the holiday and the people mean you to stay on for some reason there is nothing against it. Perhaps one of the secrets of good etiquette is, and we could coin a saying "when you start boring start going". There is a Spanish saying "fish and friends are good for three days" although this is cynical. I've known many happy stays or holidays which lasted weeks even months.

GIVE THANKS

Even if you have not enjoyed every minute when it comes to taking your leave do not forget to thank your friends profusely. It is still good etiquette after you get home to write them a newsy letter of a page or two repeating your thanks because, after all, they have taken a great deal of trouble for you. This repeated expression of thanks can be done by 'phone but a letter is more acceptable, as it can be shown to other members of the family who have contributed to the happiness of your stay:—

A sample letter:

"My stay with you was out of this world good. No holiday ever meant so much to me. No wonder you have so many lovely friends for you are a born hostess. I know one has to be careful about other people's friends but I am sure you won't mind if I 'phone Jean, who lives so near me, and ask her out. No need to write unless you would rather I did not do so.

My Brother asked me to tell you etc., etc., . . . Again, my thanks to you and Bill, you were all so wonderful,

With greetings,

Bless you,

Note:

Many people these days conclude letters "with love" or "all my love" but the word is too strong to use without discretion as a different meaning can be attached to it. For relatives or people one knows very well its use may be all right. In the plural it can usually be safely used "with our love".

RETURNING INVITATIONS

There are a number of unwritten rules in etiquette and one of them is if someone is kind enough to invite you either to a meal, party or outing, normally one endeavours to return the invitation within six months or a year.

This is not an iron rule and indeed there are exceptions. To give an example, there may be a bachelor living alone who was invited round by a married couple for supper. If we assume that it is difficult for him to return the kindness because he lives in a bedsit, then he could take a nice bottle of wine, a chicken or flowers, etc., when arriving for the meal, or ask his friends out to a meal or some other function by way of return for hospitality.

Instead of taking a gift on the day of the meal a number of people send a gift of flowers, fruit, or chocolate, next day. This is not essential but a growing custom.

Not Asking Someone Back

The unwritten idea behind return invitations is to indicate that people want to continue the friendship but if the person does not return the invitation, it could mean that they wanted to discontinue the acquaintanceship.

It all depends on circumstances but suppose that the As ask the Bs to some function and it is not returned; it does not necessarily follow that the Bs want to discontinue, although if it happens more than once it *may* be considered a diplomatic way of saying we don't wish to extend this friendship.

VISITING NEIGHBOURS

Try and 'phone first because to drop in can be inconvenient – sometimes very! It is different if you know somebody doesn't mind. Sick people, old people and children are probable exceptions because as a rule the old and the sick like to be visited. If the sick are in hospital keep to the visiting hours although if these are impossible you can try asking if you may visit at a different time and this is frequently granted, especially if you enquire nicely.

Not After Dark

Many people these days fear a knock at the door at night, so if you are going to visit a friend, do arrange the time previously or 'phone first. Even fifty years ago no one would have thought much about it but today with so much violence, care is required.

3

FORWARD PLANNING

THE KEY TO A GREAT PARTY

In the dozens of times I have been entertained only perhaps thrice have I left a party and said that it was "the" party.

It was not because the people had served champagne, caviare and smoked salmon nor because they had the biggest lounge or even that the conversation was specially witty. It was due to the hosts having pre-planned it all, not like a military operation but with care to have the ingredients of party-making right. If possible, one should go through a list of friends, and pick those who are good conversationalists and book them for your party date in advance of the "ordinary" guests. Amongst a party for 15 to 35, if you have about three or four "super" party-goers on your side to make the party great, then you should be assured of a good result.

One has to warn these friends that they will be expected to help with introductions or whatever and nothing is more important. You may even require to detail one or two good people to make sure, by introductions, etc., that a Mrs. Croft recently widowed, is not neglected. Little matters like that are essential for a great party. Others likely to need "nursing along" to help them enjoy the party (which is its purpose) are people new to the area or unlikely to know many of the guests. Its the host's job and very much good manners to be sure they are looked after and many a party fails for lack of attention to such people. Explain to your assistants which people they are to keep an eye on. Nothing may be necessary but if this worry has been delegated it leaves you free to watch for any unexpected problems. Whether the party is for children or old people matters not so long as thought has been given as to who to ask so that you do not get too many of one type.

BRING A FRIEND!

It is often done to ask a lady to bring a gentleman friend or vice versa, to a party; less often for anyone to enquire of a hostess if somebody extra can be brought along. Care is needed because it might be difficult to refuse such a request. For example, they may not have room for an extra person to stay or they may not want the person you propose to bring. Only make such requests, therefore, in exceptional circumstances and preferably by 'phone so that you can explain the reasons. It is another matter if you are on long standing terms of friendship with the host. Again, if you had just become engaged it would normally be in order to ask if you could bring your loved one along.

SOME WINE TIPS

Store wine in a cellar, dark cupboard or somewhere where it will not be disturbed. Ideally store where the temperature is about 55°F or 13°C. Avoid storing wine where there could be vibration or damp.

Wine bottles should be stored on their side so that the cork is kept moist, allowing the wine to breathe. If there is ever any sediment in red wine decant it without disturbing the sediment which is thrown away.

For every two people at a meal allow one bottle of wine; if the bottles are litres one bottle should serve three.

Some people like red wine others a white. It is nice if one can give a choice although often only one variety is offered.

Wine is poured after the starters and it is often done to have a dry white wine for the fish course and a red, white or rosé one for the main dish.

White Wine and Rosé Temperatures

A wine can be ruined if the temperature is *even 10% too cool or warm*. Champagnes, white wines, *dry* sherry, etc. are served cool, about 43°F or 6°C. To achieve this put the bottle in the lower part of the fridge for an hour or in an ice bucket for the same time. It is ideal to have the bucket near the table as in restaurants but at home one may have to bring the wine in just before serving. Don't shake the bottle; this is not medicine although it can taste like it if not handled carefully!

Red Wine Temperature

This is easier as a red wine is drunk at room temperature. Don't heat the bottle by the fire, simply decork it and keep it in the dining or living room one hour or so, not too long, before using.

Decanters

Wine decanters can be used and this conceals the type of wine! Decanting is necessary if there is a sediment which may occur especially in red wines, but only decant about an hour before using. Pour carefully and steadily so that no sediment leaves the bottle. Throw away the dregs. (See also chapter 1.)

CHILDREN'S PARTIES

Children adore parties but remember if there are grown-ups present the children should be made to behave reasonably. As a rule parties for the small ones are at tea-time with lots of soft drinks cokes or Pepsis not forgetting the usual crisps, sausages, ice-cream and cake. The tea is for parents if present. Parties are often to celebrate a birthday and guests would bring a small gift.

Many books are available to guide parents, among them being The Children's Party and Games Book, uniform with this one.

SEATING AT TABLE

With a round table there are no problems but at a rectangular table the host normally sits at one end of the table, the hostess at the other and the guests down either side.

In some rooms however it may be easier for the hostess to be seated at one side nearer her trolley or the kitchen. Where one has maybe five guests the host cannot always be at one end and the hostess at the other. There is no rule, so use discretion.

Where possible the sexes alternate round the table (married couples being separated but obviously if one is giving a party for ten people and six of them are women, use common sense in placing the scarce males – don't put one on each side of the prettiest girl which could be regarded as poor manners!).

For a bigger party it may be necessary to have two or more tables and this is suitable even if one is a small table. Thus, children if any, or perhaps two old people may have a side table, possibly with a middle aged person who is a good talker, but don't isolate the young or old too obviously or they may be offended.

One normally places the top male guest on the hostess's right while the chief lady guest would sit on the host's right, but today nobody worries at home dinners where enjoyment is the aim. If there are no special guests such as the local M.P. or other important personage put the newer friends in the seats of honour where you will be able to look after their needs best.

In old times there was some etiquette involved as to whether

Aunt Marian being the oldest Aunt of the host, sat on his right, considered the seat of honour, while the next most honoured guest sat opposite. The next senior guest would be placed on the right of the hostess and remaining guests placed in the middle. But things change and etiquette is one thing which probably alters more than most. These days it is less important who sits where, than who sits next to whom.

Far more important, is placing interesting people whom you think will suit each other in conversation as neighbours. That, not out-dated rules, is what makes a party go. It is thought unlucky to seat 13 people at table – especially on Friday the 13th!

SEATING AT LARGER GATHERINGS

For more formal meals or grander occasions seating may be arranged differently. See also chapter 7. One table may be placed at one end of the main one and is known as the "top" table. Sometimes there are other tables coming off each side of this main one or there may be a top table which seats perhaps eight to 20 people while the other tables are smaller separate ones where there may be only four or six people. It is a matter of choice and need. Where there are separate tables the bottles of wine can be placed on all the tables so that the guests do not have to move around filling glasses or waiting on a waiter to come round.

Top table guests would include the chairman, leader or most important person, any speaker, secretary, etc., if it were that kind of gathering. On the right and left in descending order of importance could be seated the people who were to be honoured but again, to a great extent this should be decided by picking those who fit in well with each other.

Wall Guest Plan

The more public the function of this larger type the more experience is needed in organising it and often guests have small cards with their names on them to show where they sit. If it is a big affair with many tables there should be a guest-plan or "map" on the wall so that people can find their seats. Where there is choice, obviously one should have a man and a woman next to each other rather than a row of men and then a row of women although the women's lib people might object! Any exceptions made for special reasons need not be bad manners. If you know that two people don't like each other for example you can then arrange to keep them apart. Between courses half way through the meal it gives fun for the gentlemen to be made to move two seats to the left.

The supreme gift of a host is his ability to place introverts beside extroverts, the quiet person next to the good talker. In brief, etiquette is more the application of common sense to ensure happy events than following silly Victorian rules.

MENUS À LA FRANCE

Many British restaurants give menus in French which can confuse. Many of us are poor French scholars and if you belong to that category, then here are two secrets, the second being the more important.

First: Memorise the following French words which will get you out of some troubles because it will tell you what sort of item you are considering, whether it is fish, fowl, etc. A knowledge of these few words will help you to make good guesses.

Second: The avoidance of panic, in the knowledge that being ignorant is no disgrace, is immensely helpful. Be calm, because it is perfect etiquette to ask the waiter, or one of your neighbours to solve your problems if, by thought, you cannot do it. Some hotels, for instance the Treglos Hotel (I believe possibly today the world's best value hotel for a quiet golfing or a pool swimming holiday) at Constantine Bay a few miles from Padstow, gives English meanings in brackets. It's all less difficult than it appears as so many French words resemble our own.

Common Words Used

Maître d'Hotel	Head Waiter
Table d'Hôte	Host's menu – set menu
A la carte	Wide choice from the menu
Cordon bleu	Top quality (blue ribbon of cooking)
Froid	Cold
Chaud	Hot
Sel	Salt
Russe	Russian
Consommé	Clear Soup
Consommé de boeuf	Clear Beef Soup
La crème de	Thick soup
Jus des fruits	Fruit juice
Fruits de mer	Seafood
Poisson	Fish
Sauce	Gravy

Poulet	Chicken
Le Lard	Bacon
Saumon	Salmon
Côtelette	Chop
Veau	Veal
Canard	Duck
Boeuf	Beef
Agneau	Lamb
Foie	Liver
Jambon	Ham
Rognon	Kidney
Cabillaud	Cod
Porc	Pork
Ragoût	Stew
Légumes du jour	Vegetables of the day
Les Pommes de Terre	Potatoes
Pomme nouvelle	Potato (new)
Le Riz	Rice
Carottes	Carrots
Chou	Cabbage
Chou-fleur	Cauliflower
Epinards	Spinach
Haricots verts	French beans
Pois	Peas
Salade vert	Green salad
Pain	Bread
Beurre	Butter
Fromage	Cheese
Fraise	Strawberry
Glacé	Iced
Gâteau	Cake
Café	Coffee
Crème	Cream
Oeufs	Eggs

4

INTRODUCING PEOPLE

AMONG STRANGERS
You introduce younger to older people.
"Mr. Young, come and meet Mr. Old."
Lesser in rank are introduced to senior in rank.
"Captain Brown, may I introduce you to Brigadier Black."
Men to women.
"George, I want you to meet my cousin, Joan Ellis."

CHRISTIAN NAMES
When introducing children to adults it is usual to call the older person "Mr." or "Mrs." (or title) and this would also be so if introducing a jobbing gardener to your neighbour. People do use Christian names quite soon enough but it is silly for Bobby aged three to begin calling a grown up "Bill" or your lady doctor "Alice". In shops and similar places Christian names would not be used with customers unless the assistant was a friend.

SECRET OF REMEMBERING NAMES
Many people especially older folk who have to introduce three or more people to other guests find it impossible to remember all the names. Here are two tricks which can be employed and a friend of mine uses the first one.

1) With a Biro he writes on the palm of his hand "John Black-Adder (eyebrows), Fiona Cranleigh-Smith (red head), Mrs. George Pot (like auntie)". In other words sufficient detail to enable you to place the people. Many times he has been complimented on his wonderful memory, whereas what he should have been complimented on was his neat small handwriting.

2)   The other alternative which can be used in emergency is to mumble or cough gently (remembering to put one's hand to one's mouth). One "gets away" with this; after all, as has been said, "the only name you remember in an introduction is your own". In such

things "Those who mind don't matter and those who matter don't mind."

MEETING PEOPLE

If you meet someone on the street, do introduce anyone with you or else say to them "I want to have a word with this person, please excuse me and wait a moment. I'll rejoin you." To just leave your companion standing neglected is poor taste. It's different in a shop where your friend could browse. If a man is at a theatre with a lady companion and someone comes to speak to her, he should stand and she can remain sitting or stand up if she wishes, and she should introduce the friend unless it is only to say a couple of words when it may be unnecessary.

INTRODUCE YOURSELF

If you are at a gathering and see someone looking shy, never hesitate to go up and say "My name is Jill White. Isn't this a nice do" or something suitable. Such a thoughtful action could make the person's day and yours! A more subtle way is to get a tray of nuts or sweets and offer them so making an excuse for conversation. Good manners are active not passive; encouraging yourself to use them will help to make life a little pleasanter for others.

5

ATTENDING PUBLIC FUNCTIONS, DINNERS, COCKTAIL PARTIES, MEETINGS, ETC.

There are special functions outside our scope. I am thinking of regimental dinners and special craft or trade functions and so on. At these affairs there may be special dress requirements and one should enquire of the secretary or a friend who is attending.

Here are a number of general points about public functions. Most people during their lives have to attend a few public functions and perhaps the most important etiquette rule is to realise that you usually have a part to play beyond merely listening to a speech, etc.

Thus at a dinner or party one essential of good manners is not to absorb one person all of the time. Everyone has likes and dislikes and sometime you may find yourself next to that "blonde" who is the girl of your dreams. Splendid, but please remember that the dear old chap on your left or right is also a guest. Except in exceptional instances, please devote some time and attention to the old boy or even the old lady beside you so that she does not feel sad and neglected.

MY PIN UP
A few years ago I was invited to a big dinner – one of those affairs where your name is on a card at the table – and after checking the guest list (prominently displayed) I discovered where I was sitting. To my delight there was a man listed next to me who, some 30 years ago, had been my pin-up and I remember considering him quite as handsome as any star of today.

In due course he arrived and I hate to confess it but my early judgement had been poor, for not only was the middle aged chap now about as ugly and gross as I have ever seen (which maybe he could not help) but he was also a sneering, sarcastic, horror. There is a moral in this story somewhere.

HANDS OUT!

At a party or anywhere, if you are standing talking especially to a lady, don't keep your hands in your trouser pockets. It is also good manners to stand erect rather than to slouch. A good appearance is a great boost to confidence so pay attention to how you dress but notice that being *over* well-dressed can have twofold rather opposite effects; firstly, it may place others less well-attired, ill at ease and secondly, people may see it as a reflection of lack of self-assurance in yourself, whether or not this be true.

FOOD AND DRINK KNOW-HOW

Food is served from the left side of a guest while drink is poured from his right. It is permissible to pass the bottle or plates of food from one guest to the next particularly where space is limited as in many small homes. These are passed in clockwise (right to left) direction.

Glasses

This is not really tricky, once again the glasses are placed on the diner's right hand and if there are several glasses one would begin with the outside one as with the cutlery working inwards. The reason for several glasses is that some people give meals with a variety of wines. They may start with a white wine and change over to a red wine. While on the subject of glasses, one should not fill a wine glass to the brim, otherwise what is called the bouquet might be lost, and also it is easily spilt. Just over half full is right.

Pre-meal Drinks

It is quite customary for people to have an aperitif and if they have not finished to bring it to the table. Such pre-meal drinks are often served until everyone arrives. They may consist of a sherry, a whisky or gin or whatever the guests request provided it is available.

Whisky of course is served in a larger, thicker glass (see the picture on page 16) and it is correct to give whisky and water, especially if you have not got any soda water handy! If mixing is left to you about 50% each whisky and water is right although some people prefer more water or request soda water, so have some in stock.

Gin is usually mixed with tonic water, lime or orange juice.

TEETOTAL DRIVERS AND NON-ALCOHOLIC DRINKS

Many people nowadays act as chauffeur for one or more others and there are always people who are teetotallers or on "the water wagon" as the saying has it, so it is necessary to have some soft drinks around. It is also an etiquette essential in case anyone is pregnant or under doctor's care, for example a diabetic. Tomato· juice is a favourite but bitter lemon, orange squash, lemonade and gingerbeer are excellent alternatives and millions have American-ized themselves to like Coca-Cola or Pepsi!

ICE BREAKERS

If you feel alone at any function and imagine that there are no other lonely people around, you are likely to be wrong. It helps to seek someone who is standing on their own and go up and talk. Before doing so, think about your approach. It could be on the weather, latest cricket score, the delicious "eats", or the news you may have heard on your car radio, e.g. "Have you heard about the new World record by . . ."

While hosts should introduce people it is not always possible and nowadays people walk up and say "My name is Bill Smith, Jean Wilson" or whatever, and either bow or stretch out a hand of welcome. It's as easy as that, but if one feels that tactic has not worked it is simple to say "excuse me" and move on. The same method is used when leaving church or even in a shop queue and many a lasting friendship has resulted.

At most parties it is considered impolite to absorb too much of one person's time, as he or she may want to circulate and meet friends.

FEW HAND SHAKES

To some extent hand shaking has been dropped, especially at parties, although in the first half of the century everyone went round shaking hands until their fingers ached. If a woman is wearing gloves she would not normally remove them when shaking hands. When introduced to one or two people, if you shake hands, do so firmly, and do look at them.

BARN DANCES AND SHOOT DINNERS

What to wear will be mainly discussed in Chapter 14. We can here mention one or two more widely held entertainments where dress matters less or hardly at all. In the country there are for example what are called barn dances and shoot dinners. These affairs are usually run by the farmer or shoot syndicate often at the end of the season. The former are for the workers and their friends while as the name implies shoot dinners are mainly run for the Beaters and the local land or farm owners, etc., by the guns who shoot. These are usually informal and people frequently come dressed in sports clothing, lounge suits or whatever they like and as a rule tremendous fun is had by all. At a shoot supper, because of jokes told while port is consumed a slight amount of sex discrimination may be indulged in, to the extent that any of the guest's wives are segregated to another room with any girl beaters, who are an acceptable innovation of recent years.

Tennis club lunches on special days are frequently given and people normally wear a wide variety of sportswear. If one is requested to bring a dish of food or cake or a bottle, the organisers who do so much work, might not like it if you forget!

6

FORMS OF ADDRESS, ENVELOPES, LETTERS, MEETINGS, ETC.

ADDRESSING

It is better to write the envelope before you write the letter and here are a few words about addressing people. There is a belief that for private use a white envelope of a squarish nature is more stylish than an oblong one. It is also thought to be better taste to use white although I do not believe it matters. So one can tell an enormous amount by looking at the outside of envelopes. While etiquette may not demand any of the things I have said above, the majority of people would judge someone to be correct if they used a white nearly square envelope for private correspondence. Even more important is what is put on the envelope and a few examples will illustrate although, here again, these are not matters of serious consequence and few would ostracise anyone for not complying with the so-called "rules"!

Addressing Envelopes

The address should be in the *bottom half* of the envelope, *and never in the top half* for the reason that the post office franking marks might partially mask the address. The stamp should be put squarely and upright on the envelope with a tiny margin left round the two sides.

The word "esquire" originally meant somebody owning land but it is still used, largely as a term of flattery and a lot of business people when addressing individuals put J. R. Blank, Esq., even though he may be a shop assistant. On the other hand this "Esquire" (short Esq.) is becoming less important and more letters are simply addressed to Mr., Mrs., or M/s being used for either Mrs. or Miss.

Personal or Confidential

It is most important to mark anything of a secret nature "personal" or "confidential" both on the envelope and at the top of the letter.

Copyright

Technically, a letter is the copyright (©) of the sender and should not be quoted without permission.

Addressing Royalty

You would write to a king or queen using the salutation "Your Gracious Majesty" but if you open with "Dear Ma'am" or "Dear Sir" as required, you could hardly be far wrong. You could conclude your letter, "I remain, your most gracious majesty's obedient servant". Royals do not die of fright over minor errors of custom.

In writing to a Prince or a Princess you could say "Your Royal Highness, the Prince of X", or simply "To Your Royal Highness, Prince John or Princess Mary". A letter could begin "Sir or Madam" and close with "I remain, Your Royal Highness's most obedient servant".

Addressing Titled People

Addressing people who are knighted is simple: Dear Sir William or if you were writing to his wife you would address her: Dear Lady Blank, and on the envelope, Sir William and Lady Blank, if writing to both.

It will be useful here to quote a few phrases and abbreviations which can be used in writing to people which have been taken from the companion Paperfront "Business Letters, Contracts and Etiquette". The subject is complicated by old rules and customs but here are the principal salutations.

DUKE	His Grace the Duke of	My Lord Duke or Your Grace (refer to as "Your Grace"). (I remain, my Lord Duke).
DUCHESS	Her Grace the Duchess of	Madam (refer to as "Your Grace"). (I remain, Madam).

MARQUESS	The Most Hon. the Marquess of	My Lord Marquess (refer to as "Your Lordship"). (I remain, My Lord Marquess).
MARCHIONESS	The Most Hon. the Marchioness of	Madam (refer to as "Your Ladyship"). (I remain, Madam).
EARL	The Right Hon. the Earl of	My Lord (refer to as "Your Lordship"). (I remain, My Lord).
COUNTESS	The Right Hon. the Countess of	Madam (refer to as "Your Ladyship"). (I remain, Madam).
VISCOUNT	The Right Hon. the (Lord) Viscount	My Lord (refer to as "Your Lordship"). (I remain, My Lord).
VISCOUNTESS	The Right Hon. the Viscountess, or The Viscountess	Madam (refer to as "Your Ladyship"). (I remain, Madam).
BARON	The Right Hon. Lord, or, The Lord	My Lord ("Your Lordship"). (I remain, My Lord).
BARONESS	The Right Hon. the, or, The Baroness	My Lady ("Your Ladyship"). (I remain, My Lady).
BARONET	Sir James Milwall, Bart. or Bt.	Sir (I am, Sir).
BARONET'S WIFE	Lady Milwall	Madam ("Your Ladyship"). (I am, Madam).
KNIGHT	Sir John Newell	Sir (between friends, dear Sir John). (I am, Sir).
KNIGHT'S WIFE	Lady Newell	Madam (between friends, Dear Lady –). (I am, Madam).

ARCHBISHOP (English)	His Grace the Lord Archbishop of	My Lord Archbishop (Your Grace).
BISHOP	The Right Rev. the Lord Bishop of, or The Lord Bishop of	My Lord Bishop (Your Lordship).
DEAN	The Very Rev. the Dean of	Very Rev. Sir (formal). Mr. Dean.
CLERGY	The Rev. William Lockwood. (If a Doctor of Divinity, add D.D.).	Rev. Sir (formal). Dear Sir, Dear Mr., or, if a D.D., Dear Dr.
JUDGE	The Hon. Mr. Justice	Sir.
PRIVY COUNCILLORS	The Right Hon. Michael Quartley, M.P.	Sir. (Yours faithfully).
MEMBERS OF PARLIAMENT	David Jones, Esq. M.P. Sir Roy Farjeon, M.P.	Sir. (Yours faithfully). Or Dear Sir.
DOCTOR or SURGEON	Dr. Peter Ransome or more politely, Peter Ransome, Esq., M.D. (A surgeon is always addressed Philip Palmer, Esq., F.R.C.S., M.D., Etc.)	Dear Sir or Dear Doctor. A surgeon, Dear Sir, or Dear Mr.

Commissioned Officers of H.M. Forces are addressed by rank, together with decorations, if any. Naval Officers, add R.N., Army Officers may have their arm of Service added, e.g. R.A., R.E.

Persons of Ordinary Rank:

TWO OR MORE MARRIED WOMEN	Mesdames
TWO OR MORE SPINSTERS	The Misses
HUSBAND AND WIFE	Mr. and Mrs. – normally no initials or (university) degrees required.
BOYS UNDER 14	Master
ONE LADY	Dear Madam

Two business women can be
addressed simply in the heading
of the letter as: Ladies

PROFESSIONAL MAN,	Dear Sir (Esq. on envelope)
BUSINESSMAN TRADESMAN,	Mr.
MANUAL WORKERS	(Mr. on envelope)
(Usually)	

Some use has been made of Chamber's Dictionary, by kind permission of the publishers, W. & R. Chambers Ltd. (The author regards this as the best dictionary for the ordinary user.)

IN A COURT OF LAW
If it is a High Court one says   "My Lord".
If it is a County Court one says   "Your Honour".
If it is a Magistrate's Court one says"Your Worship".

but if you said "Sir" it would probably not matter.

More About Titles

The top titles are king, queen, emperor or empress from which source lesser titles are derived.

As all who love or hate the lesser titles know, they are sometimes awarded for achievements or services rendered. Perhaps they can take solace from the way a medical friend once put the whole thing in perspective with his remark to me: "The pot-bellied aristocrat looks no better on the operating table than the skinny down and out."

Like tipping, titles survive and doubtless will so long as men and women are foolish enough to prize them.

Moving down from royalty we reach peers, of whom dukes are the grandest, then a fall in "class" to barons who are more common. Lower still are baronets who are mere Sirs, e.g. Sir William and Lady Black.

Addressing Doctors and Surgeons

Doctors are usually addressed on the envelope as Dr. John Blank or Dr. Blank. Strangely, surgeons who, for some reason, consider themselves a cut above doctors (no pun intended) prefer to be addressed as Mr. in the letter but on the envelope one would put John Blank, Esq., F.R.C.S. meaning Fellow of The Royal College of Surgeons and any other letters that could be applicable to the person. (The whole thing is a lot of baloney but there it is, customs are customs and they die hard.) Vets are less fussy but they probably cure a higher percentage of their patients and for many illnesses, I prefer their advice!

Addressing Others

If an M.P. happens to be a Cabinet Minister or Privy Councillor you would write "The Right Honourable" before his name (usually abbreviated to The Rt. Hon.) both on the envelope and in the name and address in the letter. On the envelope the letters M.P. would follow the name; in the letter it would be "Dear Mr. Jackson" not Dear Rt. Hon.".

Address a woman as "Dear Ms . . ." if she prefers it thus or if you don't know whether she is married. Single would be Miss.

In the case of brothers (similarly with sisters) say one is called Mr. John White, the other who is the younger Mr. George White. When *writing* to the older son you would put Mr. White (or John White, Esq.) on the envelope. When you are writing to the second or third son the correct etiquette would be Mr. George White, or Mr. James White *on the envelope.* To explain, the older son and heir does not require the Christian names but the others do, for identification especially if living or staying under the same roof. Otherwise the recipients would have to open each other's letters.

Similarly if you are writing to Mr. John Blue and his wife you would simply put Mr. & Mrs. Blue but the younger brothers would require the Christian names so as to avoid confusion, e.g. Mr. & Mrs. George Blue.

When writing for example to two or more sisters you do not require to say Miss Blank and Miss Muriel Blank, you would simply put The Misses Blank.

MEETING

Meeting Royalty

In speaking to royalty you could say "Your Majesty" but if this were repeated too often, it might be boring. Therefore, it can be changed to Sir or Ma'am which are acceptable. You would never call a king or queen Charles or Mary unless you were on close and friendly terms, that is assuming you are not a relation. In practice if you ever become friends with royalty they would ask you to use Christian names if they wanted you to do so.

The fact that the "Royal" called you Tom or Jean would not

mean that you could be equally familiar with them. The title Prince Andrew is widely used but your Royal Highness is acceptable.

Don'ts with Royalty

There is an old rule that you must not walk up to a member of the royal family and speak until they have spoken to you – as you will notice on the television.

It is easy to forget that all our royals are human and apart from a few minor items of ritual based on showing them respect, which is their due for the *risk* and work they undertake, they want to be treated normally. Royalty have a difficult time because while they are our representatives, we are really honouring the *position* rather than the person.

One custom still honoured is that you would normally never leave a function where Royalty were present until after they had gone. An illustration of this is at a race meeting no spectators go from the paddock until any members of the royal family have left it.

When the National Anthem is played you stand correctly to attention. Don't slouch with a hand in your pocket, stand with head erect and hands to the side but not rigidly which causes many people to faint.

Meeting Titled People

You would speak to a duke as "My Lord" or "Your Grace" and to his lady as "Your Grace".

Earls and viscounts can be spoken to as "My Lord" and their ladies as "Your Ladyship" or "My Lady".

A baronet is normally Sir William B...... Of course, if you are good friends first names are in order. Correctly it would be the nobleman's place to call you by your Christian or first name first.

Knights and their ladies are addressed similarly to baronets. Lots of people, even Oxford University educated, are unsure of etiquette – yet it is all easy and never a thing to lose sleep over.

Dukes, earls, baronets and all are usually as human and perhaps more modern in outlook than most of us and are probably delighted to be treated less formally than their parents were. Times change and there are a few dodos left! Of course, some snobs exist who will expect to be treated as lords but they can hardly be called the real thing.

Meeting Other People

The forms of address, when it comes to meeting people, differ. For example, in the majority of schools the pupils refer to a man teacher as Mr Jones/"Sir" and a woman teacher as "Miss" or Mrs. Name. Outside school a younger person would normally address an older person as Mr. Jones or Mrs. Smith or occasionally as Sir or Madam for strangers. A number of people use Christian names. It is the century old American method and more and more employed in this country. The rules have become more relaxed and there is a good deal of friendliness. For example even a Chairman of a big company may often be referred to as Governor or even as Mr. Black instead of Sir. In lots of businesses he may still be called by his first name, especially by old employees who grew up around the time he did.

Your boss would normally be Mr. but the American influence of Christian names mentioned above is spreading no matter how many try to delay the change. The odd job man would be Mr. as would your butcher but your gardener or gamekeeper you usually call Jimmy or Bob and your live-in servant would be Margaret or George.

There is a difficulty in some people's minds when talking to a clergyman but there is no need to refer to him as "your reverence" or to say "yes, reverend". Simply call him Mr. Smith although some people use the rather friendly term of vicar or father, or Edward.

Fifty years ago you or I might have got a smacking for calling an Aunt, Granny or Uncle by name rather than title but today many children get away happily with Christian names. It is all informal but should still be underpinned with due and reasonable respect for their elders (who in turn should take no advantage of the children on this account, which would destroy the respect).

When in restaurants when you call the waiter you can address him as "waiter" or her as "waitress" or "miss" but some would call a male waiter "steward". Probably the idea behind this is to let people know that they have been on a passenger ship! If you are on a sea cruise or flying the steward or stewardess is entitled to be called by that name or, for the latter, hostess.

An ordinary policeman is "constable" a ticket collector "collector" and a postman is happy to be called by his "trade" name.

CURTSEYING AND BOWING

When you leave a king or queen a man would bow and a lady would curtsey, before moving backwards for the first few steps. Be careful to avoid tripping over anything.

If you meet royalty anywhere, as happens at many functions, note that a man wearing a hat should doff it and bow. A woman would also bow in acknowledgement of a smile unless she was introduced, when she would curtsey.

The Americans and many other races regard this as infra dig, subservient or a sign of feudalism, but the habit has survived for royalty and all who are referred to as such, through princes, and princesses, royal dukes and duchesses. Women or young girls being presented at court tend to worry a bit over this ancient sign of respect to royalty which is all it is. They should not, for being too fussy over etiquette is almost as bad as lacking it.

Curtseying is easy. One simply moves one foot a step backwards and then bending knees lowers the body by perhaps 40 cms. or 15 inches. The head and trunk remain erect while looking at the royal person's face. In the curtsey no attempt to lower the head is required nor is there any need to drop the body forward. You are not being knighted or worshipping Allah.

Instances are known where, because of nerves, a visitor has lost balance and toppled over. This causes consternation but not to royalty whose training fortifies them against trifles. Practise a few curtseys before meeting any of the royal family.

GREETING PEOPLE – SALUTING, HATS OFF, BOWING

Men or women when introduced either shake hands, today thought of as a little old fashioned but frequently done, or else they bow. This more common acknowledgement, which is all it is, means lowering the head slightly, while looking at the person to whom you are introduced. It is merely a courteous way of letting it be known that you heard the name(s) before you begin to chat.

Saluting is a service custom of acknowledgement to superior officers, but not to sergeants or lower ranks. It is part of the method employed by the services probably as a means to instil discipline. It is presumably because of this that some people make such a palaver of it. The theory is if you do not have immediate obedience people might refuse to go into battle. Much time is spent training in saluting and any who argue about it are told that it is not a sign of subservience but that one is saluting the rank not the individual.

Among lay people, a salute is merely a friendly recognition, by a wave or twirl of the hand or arm. Of old when hats were always worn they were doffed when meeting a lady and still are but if you are bare-headed, use the salute or if you prefer, bow.

A man should not raise his hat or salute a lady till she has smiled or bowed to him. It is her privilege to invite his response.

It would be frightfully un-English to make a fuss over saluting or waving although children often bring emotion into their goodbyes and wave outrageously. They have not been made into English people yet!

On leaving friends, if it is likely to be for a time, people still shake hands but it is not etiquette to squeeze the blood out of your friend's fingers! Today, the bow and undemonstrative hand wave are taking over from the full handshake in many areas, but the old world hand grip is still around and indicates trusted friendship and good feeling. It is considered unlucky to shake hands a second time if your departure is delayed.

TO KISS OR NOT TO KISS

Customs vary in different parts of Britain. What would be seen as poor taste in Edinburgh or Cheltenham might be simply a good fun custom in Glasgow or Leeds. So varied are the views on this that a word is needed. In the South of England, when friends arrive to visit, the man and woman exchange a kiss, no more than a "peck" on the lips or cheek. It almost is a custom. All the same there are men who may be jealous of you however harmlessly you kiss their wives or sweethearts, especially men from the North and West. So be discreet. It is probably wise not even to peck a cheek the first visit. Later as one gets to know neighbours or friends better, it is different.

In the deep south of the U.S.A. is a saying "A Kiss without a squeeze is like apple pie without cheese", but they are a passionate lot in Texas. The best advice on meeting or goodbye kissing is avoid any elaborate squeezes or kisses although a slight short embrace may be acceptable.

The man should initiate the kiss with care so that if he should at any stage feel his kiss unwelcome to the lady, he will be able to draw back. It is an art which comes with experience and usually one knows instinctively if the woman is *friendly*. A kiss is usual with relatives you have not seen for a long time or dear friends.

DON'T KISS AND TELL

Be wise, be careful, never tell if the kiss is longer than it needed to be, but in so emotional a matter, be tactful. People can put meanings into embraces which one of the parties did not intend. Girls kiss each other in greeting but despite our new attitudes this is not done between English males.

7

ROYAL OCCASIONS, GARDEN PARTIES, ASCOT, PROTOCOL, ETC.

The garden parties to which members of the public are invited are those held in the summer at Buckingham Palace and at Holyrood House, Edinburgh, when the Queen is in residence for the Scottish General Assembly. Other parties are held at Balmoral or perhaps at other Royal residences. Members of the Commonwealth wishing to be invited should apply to their High Commissioner in London.

Attendance is normally by invitation but some of these invitations are available to certain institutions with Royal Patronage, the Church, Armed Services, Local Government, the legal and medical professions, etc. You could also approach the Lord Lieutenant of the County who is invited to nominate guests. Invitations are much prized and the numbers are limited.

WHAT TO WEAR AT GARDEN PARTIES

Traditionally most men wear morning dress or uniforms but *lounge suits are acceptable. In practice* both usually wear what they would wear for a wedding (their best daytime wear). Most women wear hats. An umbrella and a light mac should be taken on an uncertain day and shoes worn that fit well and will stand a good deal of walking. (There is not much shelter in bad weather and the function goes ahead regardless.)

ASCOT WEEK AND THE ROYAL ENCLOSURE

The Ascot June week provides the greatest racing in the world. There seems to be no other racecourse in this class which attracts leading people from everywhere. It is all a part of the enormous racing industry. To win a big race at Ascot is the ambition of many and winners there probably, on average, command more interest than horses which win any other European races, except the unique English Derby run at Epsom. There is a good deal of etiquette in and around Ascot – the racecourse being owned by the Queen.

It would be pointless to give exact details of who may find themselves included in the Royal enclosures as we live in a rapidly changing world but among the current rules to be followed, before you can enter the Royal Enclosure, a form has to be filled in – sponsored by somebody who has been invited several times before – which includes details of yourself or anyone else wishing to go. This must be sent in, between 1st January and 30th April and if your application is accepted you will hear in due course. U.K. residents should apply to The Ascot Office, St. James' Palace, London, S.W.1. People living abroad apply through the British Ambassador or High Commissioner.

Even those who pay for annual membership are not necessarily included in Royal Ascot week. Several of the Ascot enclosures are not open to the general public and are enclosed by railings with gates at which stewards check the badges to make sure that people have the right to enter these areas.

What to Wear at Ascot

You will also be made to promise to comply with certain clothing regulations. Details in Chapter 14. We had a streaker at Lords but who would dare do that at Ascot?

Costs

Costs change from time to time but a single day's entry to *Royal* Ascot is going to set you back the price of several bottles of whisky. If you go for all four Royal days the per day rate becomes cheaper. This is over and above all the money that, unless you are lucky, or know a great deal about horses, you are likely to lose! The entrance charge is lower at the other meetings throughout the year.

Many people lunch, eat a snack or have tea in the Ascot restaurants but some bring packed lunches and drinks which they have in the beautiful car parks. Tea at Ascot is expensive but then there is only one Ascot!

My Hat at Ascot

Nowhere in the world do the ladies dress so outrageously as at Ascot during the Royal week and what fun they give the world – desperately in need of some *wholesome* amusement.

Perhaps some of them are not quite ladies but one must remember who mothered them for many of the old aristocracy

One risk for women wearing such hats is that they could so easily fool a bee!

married beauty queens or chorus girls – probably a good thing. It brought new blood into some of the so-called blue-blooded families. The wearers of the most exciting hats and clothes during Ascot may well be descendants of perhaps some of Cochrain's young ladies (the 1930s) or ex-Monte Carlo show girls of today. Jolly good luck to them for brightening up England a little.

No matter how boldly your wife or lady friend is going to dress be sure she does not do it in such a way as to scare the horses. Unacceptable behaviour! (See also Chapter 14.)

PROTOCOL

This word means the formal or ceremonial ritual which is followed on certain occasions. It is a vast subject outside our scope but a few words may be helpful. If you are worried about the protocol for any royal occasion you can write or telephone to the secretary's department or the Press Office at Buckingham Palace, London, S.W.1. They will go out of their way to guide you on any particular problem.

ROYAL OCCASIONS

The Royal Family have garden parties at Buckingham Palace, Holyrood House (Edinburgh) or at Balmoral in Scotland. We have mentioned the dress to wear from page 61. Among other functions to which people are invited are investitures and the Queen's Awards for Achievements. There are two Awards: one for exports and the other for technology. In regard to these awards they are advertised every year in the papers explaining how to apply for them. Those wishing any other information could write to the Queen's Awards Office in London, S.W.1.

Trooping the Colour

This is a celebration for the Queen's birthday and for details one should apply to the Brigade Major, Household Division, Horseguards, Whitehall, London, S.W.1.

Invitations to the Palace

There need be no worry. The invitations reach you with full details including a map telling you to which car park you should proceed.

Invitations by royalty are really *commands* and should only be declined in exceptional circumstances but if you have to refuse the reason should be given in brief detail.

The reply is normally sent to whoever sends the invitations for example it could be something like the following:—

"Mr. and Mrs. J. R. Jackson thank Mr. X, private secretary to His/Her Majesty for the invitation to the garden party and have the honour to accept His/Her Majesty's command at Buckingham Palace at 2.30 p.m. on 4th May, 19.."

The reply should be hand-written. It need not be signed nor dated, as a date is embodied in the card wording.

If Unable to Accept

"Mr. and Mrs. J. R. Jackson thank Mr. X private secretary to His/Her Majesty for the invitation to attend the garden party at Buckingham Palace on 20th June, 19.. but cannot comply with it due to the serious illness of Mr. Jackson (*or other good reason*).

State Opening of Parliament and State Banquets

These are more formal occasions and full details of protocol will be given to all guests who arrive to watch. Britain leads the world in such functions as have been mentioned in this section. The greatest care is taken by the different authorities to make sure that all involved, especially the guests, know what they are expected to do. Wthout such attention to detail it would have been impossible, for example, for the wonderful scenes of pageantry attending the wedding of Prince Charles and Lady Diana in 1981 and televised around the world, to have been part of their happy day.

LORD MAYOR'S BANQUETS AND OTHER FUNCTIONS

There is much protocol in these ceremonies and indeed there is a good deal of it right down to the local Mayor's affairs. Among other areas in which protocol exist are regimental dinners, livery companies, university dinners and the like.

As the old established rules differ so greatly as to the type of dress to be worn, etc., it would be impossible to attempt to explain everything here and those interested should make enquiries of friends or of the people connected with the affairs.

Our public librarians are helpful and can supply reference books on almost any subject either to be borrowed or studied in the library reading room.

CHARITY BALLS, CHARITIES OR PARTIES

People frequently make up parties for these and one must explain frankly to the guests about the cost of tickets and whether the drinks are charged extra. This can save much embarrassment later, when some people are apt to forget their financial obligations. For this type of affair it is wiser to be in a party so that you and your partner are able to join a reserved table. Parties of between four and thirty are great fun at many of these big entertainments.

Sometimes people who can afford to do it will pay for their guests and this is often an ideal way to return an invitation or some other indebtedness, but usually each person pays their share.

DISPLAYING INVITATIONS ON THE MANTELPIECE

A common habit, but while many of us do it as a reminder, it should never be done for swank. It can also cause offence in a neighbourhood because someone who had not been invited might visit your home and see the invitation. This could (though it ought not to) create ill-feeling so be careful which invitations you display if any. It is probably wiser to enter them in your diary or mark your calendar.

SEATING AT IMPORTANT LARGE FUNCTIONS

There are rules of protocol for large often semi-public or charity functions so in any difficulty consult the experts. In hotels, restaurants, or banqueting rooms someone on the staff will guide you in all these matters. Space does not allow for greater details here but see also Chapter 3.

8

ANNOUNCEMENTS OF BIRTH, ENGAGEMENT, MARRIAGE, DEATH, ETC. AND LETTERS

There is an old saying which covers these as follows: "Hatches, matches and despatches". Many people announce these happenings in the papers, such as the Daily Telegraph in Britain but other papers, including local ones are widely used. Choose those most of your friends would read.

Announcements normally have to be paid for and information on the subject can be found by telephoning the relevant paper. The cost is usually reasonable. They appear in what are called the Court Pages, Announcement Pages or Social Events Pages.

We give below some examples of wordings that can be used but of course they can be altered to suit different situations. Take care to instruct the paper as to the correct heading the announcement is to go under, e.g. Golden Wedding, or Wedding!

BIRTHS

SMITH – On June 23rd at XYZ Maternity Hospital, Norwich to CHRISTINE (née Williamson)* and ANDREW a daughter (insert the baby's name(s) if you wish).

The wording can be altered if desired, for instance by adding "a brother for Jean" or " a first grandchild for Robert, Margaret, John and Betty". Provide enough information to ensure identification by readers.

---

* Née refers to the mother's maiden name.

REGISTRATION OF BIRTHS

Parents are obliged to register a birth and this must be done promptly, certainly within days, with the local registrar of births, marriages and deaths.

ENGAGEMENTS
(insert under forthcoming marriages)

MR. J. PARKER AND MISS G. WALKER – The engagement is announced between John, eldest/older/youngest/younger/ only/son of Mr. and Mrs. Michael Parker of Crawley, Sussex, and Gillian, eldest (?) daughter of Mr. and Mrs. K. C. Walker of Banbury, Oxon.

Such a notice would normally be placed by the couple or the girl's parents.

MARRIAGES
(inserted the day after the wedding usually by the bride's parents)

SMITH-JONES – On 22nd May at Oxford. Janet younger daughter of Mr. and Mrs. A. K. Jones of Melrose to David, only son of Mr. and Mrs. G. R. Smith of Worthing.

SILVER WEDDINGS, GOLDEN WEDDINGS, ETC.

BROWN-PEARSON – On 11th July, 1956 at St. Mary's Church, Reigate, Christopher John to Susan Jane. Now at Amersham.

DEATHS

MEADOW – On 9th February peacefully at Hove in his 97th year, HENRY BRUCE. Much loved by everyone. Funeral service at St. John's Church, Hove on Friday, 14th February at 2 o'clock. No flowers but donations if desired to . . . .

The insertion of all such notices, but especially those of a death require thought and care. They should be double checked for accuracy and clarity. It is wise to study several other similar notices and get the wording the way you want it to be. (See Chapter 12 "A Family Death".)

LETTERS OF THANKS

If a funeral has been attended by many people, sometimes it is wise to insert an acknowledgement in the media, especially if letters cannot be sent to everyone.

"Mrs. J. T. Wilson-Brown of The Cottage, Burgess Hill, wishes to thank all who expressed sympathy and sent flowers in her recent bereavement."

The doctor who attended the deceased, the clergyman, undertaker and any relations or friends who helped with meals, or transport should receive a short letter of appreciation. It should be hand written and if the next of kin is unable to undertake this it can be done on his/her behalf by a relation or friend.

Letters to any who send messages of sympathy can be written or printed in these terms.

"My mother, brother and I thank you very much for your condolences in our recent bereavement. It was so good of you to write so nicely about Peter. We must all now begin to rebuild our lives again."

9

ENGAGEMENTS, WEDDINGS AND CHRISTENINGS, INCLUDING GIFTS

PERMISSION TO MARRY

It is often easier to become engaged than disengaged! Once the lovers are agreed, it is a surviving custom for the man to visit the girl's father or if unavailable her mother or next of kin, to seek permission to wed. If after a little lecture about finance and the man's qualifications for looking after the girl, he is accepted, excellent. Among rich families marriage settlements or contracts may be arranged. These were common but are rare now.

In many instances, especially of mature people, requesting permission is a formality; the majority of parents would not interfere.

Sadly, and often but not always wrongly, the girl's people may feel the man is unacceptable and a quarrel can develop, or the boy's parents may object to the girl! With two people in love it is usually folly to try to prevent the wedding. Love, they say, is blind, and paradoxically the more parents strive to stop the marriage, the more likely they are to fail and the more probable it is that the couple will rush into wedlock. Such rows may split families for years or life and generally, if the two are determined, the most that "advisers" (who tend to be self-appointed) can profitably suggest is to delay a while. If the affair is destined to die away then at least time can so allow or again, the parents' fears may vanish.

Dangers of Interfering

Sometimes a passion will burn itself out in months. If it does not, it is usually better to avoid a battle you are unlikely to win. The couple are often proved right. So many parents think their child deserves a special mate, hand-picked by them. I wonder if there would be much married bliss if we all married people chosen by others. Although a parent has a duty to express fears in a reasonable way, it is probably wise to leave it at that, so be cautious of interfering. Because you brought the girl up this does not confer rights to run her life, after she is of age. She is choosing from *her* experience. Love can also be an extra eye and she may see quality in her man to which you are blind. Instinct is sometimes the best judge of character. It is similar where the opposition to the marriage comes from the man's side.

Instances occur of boys and girls in their lower teens where the boy monopolizes the girl – doubtless with her co-operation – to such an extent that her chances of meeting other boy friends are reduced or remote. In such instances of school children, it is my personal view that parents may be wise to get the youngsters to agree to go together a little less often so that each has the chance to meet others.

ENGAGEMENT GIFTS

There is a custom that when the man presents the ring to his future wife she should give him some token in exchange but this has less to do with etiquette than spontaneous kindness.

Regarding engagement rings, some prefer an antique ring or any ring with a beautiful but less costly stone rather than a perhaps scarcely visible diamond. Many who can afford a good diamond still choose this alternative. Discuss it all with a good jeweller who should be able to explain about various stones, their meanings and quality.

ENGAGEMENT PARTY

A party to celebrate an engagement is often given, when, if it has not already been publicly announced, the happy news can be released to the guests and a toast drunk to it. Warn the gathering to charge their glasses for an announcement. A toast can be drunk in any liquid, not necessarily alcoholic.

The girl's mother would normally arrange the party, to which of course the man's parents, various relatives and friends would be invited. A big party is not essential, indeed a smaller one is often preferred so that the two sets of parents may become acquainted.

CHURCH WEDDINGS, THE COST

Once a couple have agreed to marry they should decide where

they wish to be married, in a church or a registry office. If they choose a church it is normally one in the bride's neighbourhood. The vicar or priest should be contacted at the earliest possible moment to discuss the essential reading of the banns and date. Then or later, arrangements should be made about whether there is to be an organist, choir, and bells. The cost of these services including the licence and even with extras like bells is likely to total less than a third of what a reception for fifty people would cost.

Probably the majority of young girls dream of a white church wedding of whatever denomination. An important thing about a wedding is that normally the bride's parents (at least in Britain) have to pay for it. This can be a drain on finances so nowadays some people have introduced a little common sense to the situation. Heaven knows the bride's parents have enough costs with the wedding dress, reception, etc., and whether or not there is any feeling that the burden may be too great, there is no reason in etiquette why a diplomatic approach cannot be made by the bridegroom in order to help. It may be easier if any offer is made through his fiancée.

Suggestions could be that perhaps the groom or his family pay for the drinks or, for example, if a reception hall has to be hired they may be able to arrange it diplomatically at no expense to the bride's parents, but watch not to cause offence because sometimes and especially if one of the families is poor, the parents may be upset – although they ought not to be. Sharing the cost in some way, is commonly done and should not be resented.

Marriages in a registry office are usually more simple affairs and there may well be a variety of reasons why a couple choose one even for a first wedding of both parties.

Be sure to contact the authorities, if possible, months ahead of the date and time required.

DRESS

Those who can afford it will buy their own wedding dress and cherish it and perhaps pass it on to their daughters or grand-daughter or make other use of it. Nowadays a great many girls hire their wedding gown and this, if costs have to be considered, is wise.

There's an old saying "The bride should wear something old, something new, something borrowed and something blue". Worth following for it is often good to court luck. On the other hand, it is believed to be bad luck for the bridegroom to see the bride's dress before the wedding.

So far as men are concerned probably the majority hire a suit from one of the many hiring groups such as Moss Bros. but not everyone can afford this. If a lounge suit is to be worn by the groom and others officiating, the remaining guests should be told "lounge suits".

One thing is worth considering, if a man is young and likely to attend many formal weddings (count your sisters, cousins, nephews, nieces and friends) it is probably cheaper to buy a morning suit early in life as long as you get it big enough to allow for growth – growth especially at the middle, shoulders and chest. Sometimes it is possible to buy an ex-hire suit inexpensively. The cost and the nuisance of repeated hirings is saved thereafter.

THE REHEARSAL

A rehearsal can be a good plan and the clergyman who is to officiate or alternatively an experienced person in this field will usually be delighted to guide you. Remember good friends love to be asked to help and will explain such things as how in the Church of England the bride stands on her father's right but on the groom's left, and where the principal relatives should be allocated pews.

It is usual for the bride's guests and family to sit on the left side of the church while the groom's friends sit on the right. However, if there are fewer on one side, the chief usher can always re-direct guests to equalize the numbers.

A WEDDING GROUP. The father is on the left standing back, having handed over his daughter to the bridegroom. On the right is the best man, presumably clutching the ring for safe keeping. The bride's guests are shown to the pews on the left and the groom's guests to those on the right. Relations take up the front pews but there is usually a rehearsal.

USHERING

Good ushering is essential at the bigger wedding to prevent guests milling about in chaos. Few people have the opportunity of training to be an usher. The secrets are fairly simple. The usher greets the arriving guests and hands out any hymn sheets or prayer sheets available. He should greet them with a confident "Good morning", and (unless he knows the answer), "are you friends of the bride or bridegroom?". The secret of successful ushering is confidence.

Once you know to which side of the family the guest belongs you immediately indicate *firmly* with your hand "this way" and lead, *repeat lead*, the guest(s) to the pew where you wish them to be.

You should have previously been advised who are the next of kin of the bride or groom so that you can take them forward to their allocated seats.

If anything goes wrong, and this may happen, the probability is that you are the only person who notices it. The important thing not to get wrong is choosing the right mate!

WEDDING PRESENTS

Many engaged couples make a list of items which they would like and sometimes give the name of the shops where such gifts can be bought to guests who enquire if a list is available. This is a wonderful idea provided that guests tell the list organiser what they are buying, and items accounted for are promptly crossed off.

Because a list exists does not mean one must stick to it. You may wish to give some unusual item or something more or less costly than those listed. It is the thought behind rather than the value of the gift which matters. If you decline the invitation you should still send a gift. It need not be too costly; if you send a cheque it can be from as little as the cost of a bottle of whisky.

BROKEN ENGAGEMENTS

In the sad event of an engagement being broken off, gifts including the ring are usually returned to the giver; no letter is required, merely a card "with kind regards", or without any comment. All wedding presents would normally be returned to the sender.

DELIVERING GIFTS

With postage problems there is no reason why you cannot take your present to the wedding reception, especially if it is fragile. *Write or phone* to let the couple know you will be doing so and also the nature of the gift, if only to reduce the risk of duplication.

FEES AND GIFTS

This is a matter which any clergyman will explain. A licence has to be purchased and there is a standard church charge. A choir, etc. costs extra, as do bells for which there is usually a small charge. These matters should be talked over frankly with the clergyman without embarrassment so that you will know your commitments.

The vicar is usually invited to the reception and a few people give him a gift of some kind, perhaps a book token, but this is not often done. Those wishing fuller information might find Wedding Etiquette Properly Explained, another Paperfront, useful.

THE RECEPTION

After the wedding comes the reception. For big weddings this may be held in a hall within a few miles or more commonly at the home of the bride's family although flexibility is usual here. If the bridegroom's parents or aunt happen to have a larger room or a more suitable garden if there is to be a marquee, then that might be used. The guests normally file into the reception area and are met by the bride's mother first, then her father, then the groom's mother and father. The married couple should be near the middle of the room and you wish the bride well, but never congratulate her because she is supposed to have been wooed by the man, not the other way. The groom could be congratulated, the idea being that he has wooed and won.

If either of the bride's parents are deceased or not available a relative stands in for the missing spouse.

At every wedding someone should be allocated to do any necessary introductions preferably a relative who knows most of the guests. If it is a large wedding, a professional announcer may be employed as well as waiters and other staff. At a smaller wedding good friends can be buttonholed to be available to pass the drinks and see that everyone is offered food. Another task not to leave to chance is to supervise at the end of the big day to make sure everyone has got transport home.

When the bride and groom have changed into their going away things and are ready to leave, by custom and tradition confetti or rose petals, etc., are showered upon the happy couple. Avoid throwing confetti within the church grounds. Churches have to be

kept tidy and it is collectively thoughtless if the guests at every individual wedding leave a mess. There may be another wedding in the church shortly following yours. Keep confetti for the end of the reception.

It is poor taste to carry things so far as the bride's bra being filled with confetti, which is not comfortable especially on a long journey, or to load it into her bags (pun or no pun) which I saw done once.

Such things as "just married" and the traditional shoe tied on to the car are all right but it is poor etiquette when things are carried as far as they sometimes are with tyres being let down, disfiguring of paintwork (with anything which could be permanent) etc.

SHOWING THE PRESENTS

Sometimes the gifts are shown in a separate room during the reception as it saves guests returning later; on the other hand if large numbers of presents are involved the show of presents can be arranged another time specially for neighbours.

DON'T DRINK AND THEN DRIVE!

Several accidents recently have highlighted the danger for the bride and groom of a mishap while driving off on their honeymoon and it is probably wiser for them to have a teetotal driver. Whoever does drive should restrict himself to very little drink – not over one small glass. Few people are normal after the stress and strain of a wedding, so any alcohol could be upsetting and increase risk. A ginger ale, whilst looking right, is safe and there is no rule requiring a toast to be alcoholic.

WEDDING SPEECHES

This is also outside our scope except for a few comments: The standard of speeches at wedding receptions tends to be amateur and sometimes even nervous. The first speech is usually by the bride's father or perhaps an uncle or cousin of the bride, or rarely the officiating clergyman. The danger of this type of speech is that it does not end before everyone wishes it had, so unless you are brilliant, keep it short. A couple of little stories about the bride's previous life, perhaps some comments about her beauty even if it is not too obvious, and a few words on how lucky the groom is should suffice. The speech should not bore as they are sometimes apt to do. The best way to avoid boring is to test your speech on some uninvolved third party who can help you sharpen it up.

The second speech should be a reply by the bridegroom. The guests do not expect the bridegroom to make a brilliant speech so he has nothing to worry over and if he is a little shy or inexperienced, let him keep it brief. A friendly audience is easily spoken to and all he need do is to thank his parents, perhaps for their foresight in having him, and her parents for providing her but one way or another to express gratitude to the old folks including any surviving grandparents. Next he can thank the best man for the wonderful way he has prepared him for the occasion. Finally, of course, he must not forget thanks for the presents and he must end by toasting the health of the bridesmaids. The bride may also say a few words if she wishes. This reminds me of the story of the wife who always gave her man the last *two* words: "I apologise." Many of the speeches end with an invitation to the guests to visit the couple's new home, but not all at once.

Following on this, the next speaker is usually the best man who replies on behalf of the bridesmaids (later they can each be given a small present) and says a few words about the groom's previous life. Any leg pulling of the groom should be harmless. He has to be careful not to offend any of the relations or to allow too many cats out of the bag. This is not the stag party!

The best man or someone often arranges an evening party or entertainment for the bridesmaids, ushers, etc., if desired. If guests are travelling long distances to the wedding, somebody should be detailed to arrange overnight accommodation, perhaps in a hotel, for those requiring it. In certain circumstances such guests might be included in any evening party or entertainment.

THE STAG OR HEN PARTY

My only comment on this ancient custom is to try to hold back on the amount of liquor consumed! Years ago these parties were held the day before the wedding but fortunately the custom now – in view of the risk of excess – is to hold them a few days earlier. Although few mind if a stag party is omitted the fact remains that plenty of people go in for them. From a medical viewpoint there is probably nothing worse for a bridegroom than to have been drunk a day or few days before he gets married. It is usual for costs to be shared among participants.

In a similar way hen parties – a fairly recent innovation for the girls – have become popular in our more affluent society and similar comments apply.

CHRISTENINGS

As the name implies this is a religious ceremony but the services of a clergyman are not all that is required. It is well for parents to make sure they are acquainted properly with the religious implications of this solemn ceremony for their child and how its future upbringing will be expected to fall in line. For the less devout some inquiry and study may be the order of the day.

In the Church of England one would consult the clergyman beforehand so that all the details can be arranged. There are no special clothes required for the ceremony of baptism. Those who attend do so in what used to be called their "Sunday best" usually a lounge suit. The clergyman will show the various people attending where to stand and any godparents should all be present. In the Church of England a boy would normally have a minimum of two godfathers and one godmother while a girl would have two godmothers and one godfather. In the Roman Catholic Church one or more godparents of each sex is the rule.

These godparents must be Christians and they promise to undertake religious duties concerning the child and are responsible for doing their utmost to see that the child is brought up in a Christian way. Be sure to invite them in good time but if one is ill, a proxy is acceptable. All good godparents remember to send birthday cards and perhaps a gift till the child is adult or longer. They should also do their best to be sure that eventually the child is confirmed in the church. It is normally the custom to hold the Christening service when the baby is about six to eight weeks of age.

In the Church of England a godmother holds the baby and at the moment of baptism she hands it on to the left arm of the clergyman but of course in different churches various other customs prevail and that is why it is essential to consult with your clergyman first so that nothing goes wrong on the day. After the short, simple service, the father can, if he wishes go back to his pew for the rest of the service while the mother and her baby would be taken home. Christenings can be held at home but it is considered nicer to be in a church.

Giving the Christian Name(s) to the Clergyman

The names should be spoken clearly to him beforehand or perhaps for safety he could be previously supplied with the name(s) on a slip of paper or card. Care is needed here because some elderly clergymen may have poor hearing. There is a classic story of a time when twins were baptized. The clergyman misheard the names of Kate and Sidney and the children were baptized as Steak and Kidney!

Gifts for Babies

It is customary for relations or friends of long standing who are present at the Christening to give a small gift. A girl might receive a piece of jewellery, perhaps a brooch or a bangle but there is a lot to be said for giving some Savings Certificates. A boy might receive a Bible, prayer book, silver spoon or, again, money gifts for some form of saving. The presents need not be big as they are only tokens.

Following the Christening the group generally return to the parents' house or some suitable home for a reception where tea and some food is served. A more elaborate meal can be arranged – it is a matter of choice but not necessary. It is acceptable simply to have tea and an iced Christening cake. Remember to ask the clergyman and his wife along.

One of the most important things about the baptism is the choice of the name because there is no question that names affect people for life. I would hate, for example, to be called Jezebel. People somehow do tend to become like their names! There is something to be said for sticking to old family names and if two names are given one can be taken from the family while the other perhaps can be more modern. Later in life the child may prefer to use his second name. Another matter to watch is that the initials may form words. For instance if your surname was Thomson and you called your son Robert Arthur, I hate to tell you that he would be called Rat or Ratty at school, and maybe for life. Henrietta Hogg could end up as "Greedy" while Anne Teak might find herself invited out only by old fashioned men! The companion book to this, BABIES NAMES A to Z gives some 3,000 from which to choose.

The custom of calling boys after their fathers is usually unwise. Even if the child has a middle name, if there is a John R. Smith and a John S. Smith at the same address, letters, messages, bank accounts and the like are sure to get confused – not to mention tax assessments!

10

GREETINGS MESSAGES

TELEMESSAGES

The Telemessage, fifty words, but more if wanted, can be telephoned or telexed and charged to your account/'phone number, for delivery the next working day.

For such greetings messages you can request delivery on an attractive appropriate card. They are quite expensive but so much nicer than a letter. Things which create pleasure usually cost money! Such messages should be telexed or 'phoned (you *can* use a payphone) before 10 p.m. (7 p.m. on Sundays) *the day before delivery is required*. In my view it's worth allowing for hiccoughs in the advertised speed of the system and to ensure arrival in time for a Saturday wedding, deal by Tuesday, or, latest by Wednesday afternoon. They are marvellous for weddings, birthdays, the birth of a baby, coming-of-age 18 or "again" at 21 and anniversaries of weddings, etc.

People living abroad should telephone or visit their local Post Office or Cable Office and enquire how to link in their message to our U.K. telemessage service. If you want to send a telemessage overseas, ask your telephone operator for "international telegrams".

As the wedding greetings are usually *read out* amusing wording can be thought out:

To a boxer: "Don't knock her out."

To a gardener: "Keep your rose blooming."

To anyone: "May you have the wisdom of Solomon,
       the patience of Job
       and the children of Israel."

To a stockbroker: "Share and share alike for the best dividends."

To a banker: "Keep up the interest rate."

To a lady nurse: "You've got your hands full now."

To a farm manager and his bride: "The bull bellows but remember
    where the milk comes from."

To a lady doctor: "Don't be an anti-body now."
To a man who marries his secretary: "He's not the boss now."
To a timber merchant: "Obviously someone knew a good deal."
To a Scotsman: "It's all free now."

11

DIVORCE

Punch's single word advice to those about to marry was "don't". This word could almost but obviously not quite be applied to people considering divorce, particularly if there are children. The results of divorce where there is a family are often disastrous and expensive for both parties, frequently for the one who expected to receive money. The legal profession benefit greatly, a point to remember if the solicitor is encouraging you over much.

Among the rubbishy views held are that rows help a marriage. You might as well believe that banging your head on a wall so as to enjoy the relief when you stop, is healthy.

TOO MUCH SEX EQUALITY

Possibly much of the increase in divorce these days follows the argument for sex equality which seems to encourage rows which can destroy love. For in spite of all theories, observation confirms that, if people are quarrelling and coming to blows, love tends to diminish. All the sadness, distress, financial ruin and so on which can accompany divorce should mean that perhaps if some ideas can be given here this great unhappiness may be avoided. The advocates of easier divorce rarely warn us of the bitter price. Of course, sometimes, divorce is the reasonable course and this possibility must be respected by both parties if amicable arrangements for it are ever to result.

END QUARRELS

It must be remembered to end a quarrel usually one side must give. The moment a row develops then one of the partners has to act fast. An almost invaluable help in such situations is for either partner, usually the stronger willed one, to take a low profile in the middle of the affray and back down by yielding much, if not all. It isn't easy but is usually the only way.

The best advice is of course the oldest in the world, "forgive and forget" and try to completely bury the subject of the quarrel which is often over such a trifle that people cannot even remember what it was about half an hour later. Harping or nagging on and on will pave the path to the law courts.

THINK OF THE CHILDREN

Divorces which occur before a child has arrived are probably less serious although one or both partners may feel crippled emotionally for a long while afterwards and this "cost" is hard to quantify. Few would condemn others for failing in what is a difficult relationship to sustain over a lengthy period, yet to achieve a happy co-operative, loving marriage is something for which a couple may still feel proud to strive.

The little concessions and kindnesses of life are terribly important when living together and that is why good manners are one of the sources of lasting happiness. The little gifts a couple present to each other, whether it be a few flowers for the wife or only a few ounces of fudge prepared for her husband, help to make a marriage tick over smoothly. The valued gift is that which requires effort on the giver's part. Causes of misery after the first few years are so varying only those under the heading of good manners can be stressed.

Without overdoing it or becoming too fussy a marriage is usually helped by frequently expressing the simple things, remembering to say, "thanks", "good morning sweetheart", even to pass the butter unasked, all play a part in a good marriage. If one party got the breakfast but forgot the marmalade, instead of blame, how wonderful is the offer to get it. There are compensations in most things and the reward for pulling together with a smile is beyond price.

I remember a husband being upset because he had broken the cork and some of it got into the wine when the couple had important guests to dinner. One of the guests turned the mishap into victory as he explained that it had recently been discovered this happening improves the taste of the wine! Laughter! Tact may be more necessary in marriage than outside it.

Consideration for the children when a divorce is to happen should have a high priority. People who once loved each other and were capable of that, but have had enough and can't continue should force themselves to switch from their own problems to the ones they will create for the children. It must be realised that bad as the situation is for the mature. It may be a dozen times worse for an innocent child if he or she in practice becomes a one parent (or one parent at a time) child, feeling lost in a usually hard, cruel world.

Even at this stage, when the enormity of divorce and its ramifications strikes, it may not be too late for reconciliation. Never allow pride to block wisdom. In life those who pull back from the brink rarely regret it. Swallowed pride is a good health food.

AFTER A DIVORCE

Even if one party feels innocent and bitter due perhaps to continuous unfaithfulness, or alcoholism, they should try to get round to forgiving and forgetting what has happened, for the sake of the future but particularly because of any children. Being human we are not perfect and some people find it harder to forgive, because of their nature. Ironically it is themselves they often finish damaging most.

Goodwill on both sides will help to mitigate what may be frightful consequences.

In passing it might be mentioned that many marriages have survived a period of unfaithfulness. Recent research indicates that a percentage of men and a smaller percentage of women have been unfaithful yet their marriages have remained happy even when this was known to the partner.

A FEW IDEAS ABOUT DIVORCE WORTH THOUGHT

A point people don't always grasp is that although the solicitors might say to a wife who is getting a divorce that she will be able to obtain a lot of maintenance money they may forget to explain that if the man goes bankrupt, takes ill, dies or even more likely vanishes to another country or is unable to pay, then she and the children may be poor. Responsibilities towards them, depending on their ages, may restrict her ability to take over the breadwinning as well, or the years spent bringing up a now mature brood may mean further career prospects are slight indeed.

A wife may receive alternatively an outright sum of money in settlement but due to the dangers of inflation, this is no real guarantee of income either.

12

A FAMILY DEATH

When death occurs close to you it is recognised that the majority of people, especially widowers or widows, are temporarily going to be in a combined state of shock, confusion, distress and possibly fear. In such circumstances the only good advice is, so far as practicable, leave the funeral arrangements which must be made to the professionals. For many people a death in the family is a new experience as they may have been young when other deaths occurred and probably the best advice is as follows:—

SEEK DOCTOR'S HELP

Keep closely in touch with the deceased person's doctor who should give you help regarding urgent matters such as the death certificate (two certificates needed for a cremation) and how they are dealt with in law. Only a few days are allowed for registering a death.

Sudden deaths are common and in law a post-mortem may have to be held. This is not generally a cause for alarm and your doctor will make the arrangements.

CONTACT FUNERAL DIRECTOR

Immediate action is required to contact a funeral director, especially at times of the year such as March when usually more people die than any other month. It could be wise to anticipate the death by consulting the funeral director *in confidence* when death is thought to be certain within days. If the invalid survives no harm is done.

THE CLERGYMAN

The clergyman must be called at once regarding the funeral arrangements because all three people mentioned here have the difficult job of dove-tailing the arrangements and dates to fit in with each other.

POINTS TO BE STRESSED

As indicated above all the matters are apt to be so involved that you simply must place your confidence at this time in these people, the doctor, the funeral director and clergyman. If you have a family grave a good funeral director will make the proper enquiries and clear any authority required.

A FAMILY GRAVE?

If there is no family grave then the funeral director will have to arrange for what is called a "lair" or burial plot to be purchased.

CREMATION

Alternatively if it is to be a cremation then two doctors will be required to give certification (the deceased's doctor will help here). Times and dates will need to be arranged with the crematorium officials and one's own vicar to conduct the service. The funeral director can help here and make these arrangements. It is always wise in such matters to have all dates and times *double checked*. There is a need for speed and urgency until the arrangements are fixed even if the funeral may not take place for several days.

THE KEY MOURNERS

Some of the mourners may have to come by air and those who are taking part in arrangements at the funeral will have to be invited either by letter or telephone. Confirmation will be needed that they are available and can come at the time fixed. A card showing any duty to be performed should be given to those officiating.

Where one is not a relaton it may be acceptable for one person representing the family to attend the funeral, rather than several. It is important to explain this to the bereaved family beforehand or afterwards so that no feelings are hurt. If the friendship is close the other members should send a joint letter of sympathy or individual letters. (See Chapter 21.)

Inserting the announcements (see Chapter 21); here again the funeral director can arrange for the insertion of an announcement in the national or local papers, arranging to pay for it and charge it to you later.

Among other things the funeral director will arrange are flowers, transport of mourners, possible accommodation or meals for some of the people.

WREATHS OR SPRAYS

It is the custom to arrange for a florist to deliver any flowers you send. Some mourners, however, may wish to take their own flowers bought from the florists or make a bunch or spray of garden flowers. Others may like to make a wreath and if they are taking it to the church they can arrive early and lay it near the other flowers at the graveside.

The important thing is to tie a card to the flowers saying who has sent it and with the words "with love" or perhaps "Till we meet again" and the names of those who have given the flowers.

AT THE SERVICE

In the church the chief mourners would usually be seated in the right-hand front pews. The next of kin would be nearest the aisle and these mourners would be dressed in black or dark clothes if possible. For other mourners today the colour need not be so dull, blue, brown, etc., being seen, men usually wear a black or dark necktie and women sometimes a veil. Black armbands are still worn in some parts of the country.

Occasionally, services are held in a home.

INVITATIONS

There is usually no invitation for the general public to a funeral other than the press announcements. Relatives or close friends should be telephoned or told by letter as should any old friend whom it was felt would like to know but might not have seen the notice.

MEMORIAL SERVICES

Today, especially where there is to be a crematorium service, it is becoming common to announce "funeral private, Memorial Service later" (to which friends or neighbours are invited by press announcement or, relations or old friends, verbally or by letter).

EMBALMING

Embalming or partial embalming would be discussed with the funeral director.

PLACE OF BURIAL OR SERVICE

The deceased may have expressed a wish to be buried in a certain place or to have a funeral service conducted at a particular church and may even wish a certain clergyman to take the service. If any such requests have been left in writing, out of respect for the dead, these wishes should be complied with if possible. I say "if possible" because there may be a reason such as expense why such wishes are not practicable as conditions may have changed.

COST OF A FUNERAL

This is one of the most serious costs that can hit a family. Even the cheapest funeral may run to several hundreds of pounds while if one includes a headstone of good quality the cost may leap to four figures easily. On top of all this is the standard fee for the church and choir and any wreaths will add to the total bill. If no family grave has been purchased a plot will need to be bought. Then there are the costs of the announcements and the funeral cars depending on how many are required to travel to the cemetery.

Discuss Cost Frankly

Solid oak coffins are expensive but one that looks similar to oak is cheaper and other types of coffin come in at lower prices. At this sad time no one wants to sit down and discuss the odd few pounds yet anyone who has the slightest problem about the expense of the funeral should not fear to have a talk with the funeral director. These men have great experience and obviously recognise that a family from a small house with a second-hand car would expect to be charged less than the wealthy nationalized chairman's wife, who may want one last big show of efficiency!

Any good funeral director will be happy to give an approximate estimate which will enable you to assess whether some savings could be made. For example neighbours may offer to use their own cars instead of travelling in the limousines. The funeral director will explain how costs can be reduced.

RETURNING TO NORMAL

Sad and frightening as a death might prove, everybody should aim to get back to their normal lives as quickly as possible. Those who have passed on would not expect their deaths to be mourned forever and this must be surely the best advice.

WIDOWS WHO BORE

And widowers of course, but as there are fewer of them, we have mentioned widows first. Although life has to go on many people who have lost their husband or wife appear to be incapable of talking about anything else for years and years. The temptation is enormous. Frequently an older person is left alone in the family home where naturally their thoughts tend to centre around the person with whom they have spent maybe thirty to sixty years.

From the health and happiness viewpoint, it is essential to try and take up some hobby or throw oneself into some work, perhaps of a charitable nature, which may help to reduce the pressure of sad and negative thinking and will also bring in some new ideas likely to cheer the person up. It may be better to move maybe to a smaller house nearby. For older people to go far away could be unwise. Young widows may find it surprisingly helpful for them to try and find a job fairly soon.

Neighbours are usually good provided the person does something to help themselves but naturally people are not willing to go on inviting you to their parties, outings or trying to obtain membership for you to join a group if you don't make an effort to help yourself. Once again this is a question of thoughtfulness for others, which is at the root of good manners.

When one is feeling low and imagining others are being selfish and lacking in consideration for you, reflect for a moment, on whether there is not a lot more you could do for yourself. Relations, friends and neighbours can help you for weeks or months, but for life each of us must try and readjust ourselves as well as we can.

WILLS

Wills can be complicated or easy and books exist showing how a will can be drawn up. The point for this book is that people should develop what can be termed a proper will philosophy. That is members of a family ought to realise there have been more quarrels over wills than almost anything. There have been rows lasting years, parents not speaking to children for decades over the division of what is left by someone who has died. Another source of disagreement may be caused by people trying to make others change their will or who have been pressing to force someone to make a will.

The right approach, usually, is for us all to accept that the person making the will can leave their worldly goods to whom they wish, although a surviving spouse and certain relatives if cut out or unfairly treated, can make legal claims which may succeed. Not only out of consideration for others is it generally unwise to quarrel over such matters but doing so frequently has the opposite effect to that which the person causing the quarrel wants. Angered people, not being saints, can be vindictive.

Reflect that the majority of wills do not cover large sums of money other than the family home and even the family home is often still partially on mortgage. What the rumpuses are frequently about, is what are called the chattels. Someone worries over a silver tea platter or an argument develops as to whether Aunt Bessie intended her nephew to have the clock.

Those concerned should remember that the value of most of these chattels, in comparison to the total estate value (including a family home) is usually small. It is not worth arguing about such matters and risking any lasting resentment. Such items are usually valued for tax and there are ways in which disagreement can be avoided. For example a "pecking order" can be worked out; that is, after valuation for probate, it might be arranged that the next of kin has the first choice, then the next in line, the second choice and so on. Or perhaps the order of choice could be by age, allowing the younger generation the first pick following on to the older people. Obviously, if a cousin or a brother wanted a particular item a request could be put in and considered by the other beneficiaries but whatever happens, people should decide against ill feeling.

After using such a method of dividing any chattels, each person reimburses the estate according to the *value* of items they are having. This adjustment means that, financially at least, all beneficiaries can feel fairly treated.

Altering Wills

Quite often depending on the age of people, etc., alterations can be amicably arranged by friendly discussion ready for solicitors to make the amendments in correct legal language. One thing should be remembered, many people are sensitive about wills and about their personal affairs and it may be bad taste or illegal to try and force people to do things they do not want to do.

In the old days a great many wills tried to tie money up in trust thinking of it as "family money" and sometimes people tried to tie such money up for generations often with disastrous results. Fortunately nowadays such complicated wills are generally avoided. It is a different matter where a trust may have to be formed for the protection of young children in a family. These trusts only tie the money up until children are 25 or some other age depending on circumstances.

Enough has been said to alert readers to some of the problems. In an ideal world it might be that people should openly discuss their affairs but many prefer not to and such views should be respected.

13

INVITATIONS AND REPLIES TO INVITATIONS

The majority of invitations are made be telephone because that way you get a quick answer and it can be cheaper! The secret of success is, if there are more than one couple being invited first try and book those who are likely to be engaged or who are away from home a lot. Where however, a number of invitations have to be sent out in advance and replies required, especially for important functions, such as weddings, charity balls, celebrations, christenings and the like, then they should go by post or by hand delivery.

It is correct to invite people by an ordinary letter but it is easier to use post cards. Normally invitation cards go in white envelopes. Some people love to display these cards on the mantelpiece and they are also less likely to forget the date.

INCLUDE A MAP

In sending an invitation to anyone who may not know the area, draw a map showing how to reach you or have a simple map drawn and run off a few on a duplicator or photocopy some as it is a tremendous help and a sure sign of kindness to your friends.

Here are some invitations which would be written or typed on a card unless the partly printed ones are used.

Card invitations are usually in the third person, as shown on page 94.

The invitation should show whether it is dinner, or less formal or whatever. If the words "black tie" are on the invitation it means that a dinner jacket should be worn and implies a formal occasion such as a dinner or dance. (See Chapter 14). The telephone number should be included if 'phone replies are acceptable.

Mr. and Mrs. John Jackson

invite

Mr. and Mrs Ivor White

to a Bridge Party and Buffet Supper at 7 p.m.
at 21 Beech Road, Brighton
on Friday, 8th August

21 Beech Road,
Brighton,
BN40 6XY   R.S.V.P.

or

John and Mary White at home

on Thursday, 28th June

Cheese and Wine Supper
7.45 p.m.

9 The Elms
Reigate,   R.S.V.P.
Surrey   Tel. Reigate 4312

Here is a wedding invitation, and it is usual to have these printed
on card.

Mr. and Mrs. John Smith
request the pleasure of the company of

. . . .

at the marriage of their daughter

Jane Margaret

to

Christopher Jones

at

St. Mark's Church, Eden Street, Morden,
on Saturday, 4th April, 1999, at 2.30 p.m.
and afterwards at the Three Lions, Morden

5 Avenue Road
Morden
Surrey (post code)   R.S.V.P.

INVITATIONS WHICH BENEFIT CHARITY

Nowadays fewer dances, dinners or parties are given privately. Many people have numerous cards on their mantelpieces but if you examined them you might find some were in aid of charity. Such invitations may be more expensive than they look because you may be expected to become involved in auctions, raffle tickets, annual subscriptions to the charity, etc. Be warned!

REPLYING TO INVITATIONS

It is not *always* necesssary to *write* a reply to invitations other than weddings, 21st birthday parties, etc. For small functions where you are close friends it is usually all right to telephone.

Where something is being arranged for a club or a dramatic society with many members, replies should be sent by letter or card (posted or delivered) to enable the secretary to plan.

Sample replies, usually given in the third person:-

> Mr. and Mrs. Arthur Wood
> accept with pleasure the kind
> invitation of Mr. and Mrs. Hay
> to the wedding of their daughter, Clare,
> on 4th September and to the reception.

(Such cards being in the third person require no signature.) Alternatively:

> Mr. and Mrs. Arthur Wood regret that,
> owing to a previous engagement,
> they are unable to accept
> Mr. and Mrs. Hay's kind invitation
> to the wedding of their daughter, Clare.

No explanation need be given but it is kind to enclose a short note with the reply explaining why, or it can be included (as shown) on the card. The reply can be a letter.

Special invitations may need special replies, e.g.

> date, address and phone no.

Dear John,
    It was kind of you to write asking me to stay a fortnight with you in Auckland and I accept with delight. I have made enquiries and find I could be in New Zealand during June or

July and if you agree this is a good time of year please pick any date you like and airmail me and I will comply with your wishes as to the dates that suit.

It really was kind of you to think of this because I have never been as far from home and I am looking forward to seeing you immensely.

Very sincerely,
signature.

The letter can be longer to include any interesting news.

14

THE RIGHT DRESS FOR THE RIGHT OCCASION

FUNERALS

Fashions change rapidly. Most of us have at some time arrived at a function incorrectly dressed. One reason is that customs vary in different parts of the country. At the time of writing for example people in Scotland regularly attend funerals in morning clothes if they have them, or, if not, in dark suits and ties.

In the South, special occasions apart such as the burial of the famous, one rarely sees a morning suit unless worn by undertakers and not always then. Fortunately life is less formal now and again the message is don't worry if you are dressed a little differently. Does it matter? Reasonable and decent behaviour is the hallmark of etiquette. Manners, not dress, make the man.

One message for this chapter is never hesitate to ask a friend whom you think would know if in doubt. No one goes to a funeral dressed in a track suit – a lounge suit is usual. Women, apart from next of kin, don't always wear black in many parts of Britain, but dress sombrely.

Those who are invited to funerals which are special occasions may have to hire a black morning suit.

WEDDINGS

Social standing has some bearing on how one dresses but do not worry so long as you use discretion. Probably most who attend weddings in a morning suit and topper hire them from stores which provide this service. Guests can get away without the top hat. The wearing of morning dress is widespread. It can be black or grey, although the rich may have two suits – one for funerals and the grey for weddings. To wear the black at a wedding is correct, but the tie should never be black.

At most, except stylish weddings – some men are in lounge suits but it adds "style" if the ushers, groom and best man are in morning dress. The secret, if a secret, if one arrives a little wrongly dressed for any occasion, is not to give it a thought. Probably nobody else will.

A white wedding for the bride whether in a church or a registry office is a must for many girls. Some brides borrow a bridal gown or there may be one "in the family". Others will buy a dress, which with minor alterations, can be used for other purposes maybe a big dance. An alternative is to hire.

RESTAURANTS, ETC.

A few have rules that one is *only* allowed in if "properly" dressed. Men without a tie can't enter some places, a few require lounge suits and once, years ago, a clergyman (it's true) stopped my friend Margaret entering his church, because she had no hat. She asked if it would be all right to lay her handkerchief over her head, but "No". He did in the end allow her to pull her skirt up over her head, leaving only flimsy undies on show. Everyone laughed.

SPORTS WEAR

People are still fairly strict over sports clothing and members of tennis or cricket clubs are expected to wear white; there is no doubt that it raises the "tone" of the game although many who play tennis nowadays wear jerseys or a scarf of some other colour and this is usually acceptable provided the main sportswear is white. Acquaint yourself with the custom of the club and area in which you play. Where there are all-weather courts people play in cold weather in track suits or other suitable attire with a variety of colour (see also Chapter 16)

DANCING, COCKTAIL PARTIES, ETC.

As dress is to some extent based on what the man wears I deal with this first. A generation ago most came to drinks parties in dark suits but not today. The lounge suit of any reasonable colour is correct but people come in a variety of clothes. In most areas a man can arrive in a sports jacket and the younger generation often wear jerseys or casual clothes. However, this would not apply to an early evening business function where lounge suits would normally be the order. Black shoes match a dark suit, while brown may be better with most other colours. If it is very hot at a party men should ask the hostess if they may remove their jackets; but in the U.K. braces are "out". (Women should be careful what they remove.)

Women's attire is another matter as greater care is needed. At some smart parties no one minds the girls arriving in the most modern slinky pyjama suits, including "cleavage" but those who might be shy would feel happier in less trendy wear. Anyone who is uncertain of the correct dress can always ask the hostess when accepting the invitation and this is important as what is worn can often set the tone. We have all seen some of the modern fashion models on television but no one should strut about the way they do – that would be bad taste – drawing excess attention to oneself.

At some dances "black ties", that is dinner jackets are requested. "White ties and tails" are rare now.

ROYAL ASCOT

In the Royal enclosure the male guests wear morning dress; outside of the Royal enclosure it is acceptable to have suits and of course the ladies can exhibit their headgear as much as they like. Many men wear a rose or carnation, in the Royal enclosure or in the paddock area outside it.

Ascot is notorious for occasional downpours of rain and in their own interests women are probably wise to avoid dresses which trail on the grass.

The male suits (morning dress) are like those worn to weddings and include a grey top hat (essential), a morning coat and grey or striped trousers. A waistcoat is necessary and of course a tie, usually a grey one. This is similar to what is worn to important funerals and still in some parts of U.K. and on state occasions. Many men go to Ascot in the darker funeral suit and hat but if you have both, then wear the grey one.

There is no question that many of the girls and women who attend Ascot take a great deal of trouble with their appearance. One could hardly say that all of the results are beautiful and they can even be shocking. Hats can vary in size from little larger than a thimble to enormous things several feet wide. It all adds fun and gaiety, if not to those wearing them in some of our British weather, at least it puts on a show for television and press. In the *paddock area*, morning dress is not essential and many wear lounge suits. (See also Chapter 7.)

THE DERBY

The sport of kings would not be what it is without the Derby. Here, if anywhere, all men are almost equal because they can all come away penniless. This great British sight of perhaps a million people spread over Epsom Downs plus hundreds of bookmakers has to be seen to be believed. Apart from the grandstand area everyone is dressed exactly how they like with open-necked shirts and, sadly often, with raincoats and umbrellas. The grandstand area has some sections only open to club members with special tickets and in these "aristocratic" areas some men wear top hats and tails and the ladies all their finery. Thirty years ago a third of the people wore morning dress, today the percentage is less.

For those watching in the paddock area, apart from looking at the horses one of the attractions of Ascot and the Derby is the chance to see the sovereign and members of the royal family. It is one of the good old-world customs that as the Queen passes near or arrives in the paddock, men wearing hats take them off for a moment and if by chance (as happened to the writer) one walks straight up to the Queen, a *slight* curtsy or for a man a bow is correct as one stands aside to allow her to pass.

COVENT GARDEN

Times have changed and people attending the opera and ballet now wear what they are most comfortable in. Gone are the days of opera top hats, cloaks and beautiful dresses (almost).

GLYNDEBOURNE

Those wishing to attend the operas which take place between May and August each year at Glyndebourne should apply to Glyndebourne Opera House, Glyndebourne, Lewes, Sussex. People take picnics, dress in dinner jacket and black tie, short or long dress is customary but not obligatory. People wearing jeans and sweater will be turned away.

WIMBLEDON

No matter what problems the authorities at Wimbledon have with the players a few words are not out of place here for the spectators.

People today go to Wimbledon dressed in almost anything

except in the special stands and areas restricted to the debenture shareholders where they seem to dress less outrageously and with a little more decorum than ordinary sports fans.

The main point to be stressed for spectators is that Wimbledon has a tradition of good sportsmanship and no one would expect hooliganism at this arena. With changeable weather conditions it is wise to take a mackintosh or other protection and, in case it is cold, gloves and a scarf.

GOLF

People wear almost anything for golf but obviously sports clothes are best. In the old days most people wore what were called plus-twos, later, a plus-fours suit but this has largely disappeared and the majority now play in coloured jerseys and trousers. Women wear a sports or trousers suit. Don't forget golfing shoes and no high heels! If a spectator you may need warm clothes.

SHOOTING AND BEAGLING.

Most shooting men these days go dressed in some sort of shooting jacket specially lined to protect against the weather. The majority wear sports trousers but ordinary old lounge suit trousers are in order because the lower part of them is usually tucked into gum boots which are often worn. In the early months of the season if the ground is dry one can shoot in ordinary country shoes. The majority of regular *guns*, as they are termed, wear long stockings over trousers, knickerbockers or plus-twos. A hat is essential for a shooting man, as camouflage, and almost any type from a trilby to a cloth cap can be worn. Guns with good hair *may be* forgiven if they forget their hats.

Therefore if you are asked to go as a guest to a shoot you can go dressed in almost anything with a country flavour. Women would normally be dressed in a tweed suit or a husky jacket but do remember to take strong shoes or gum boots. Avoid white or any colour which would scare the birds away.

It can also be cold, especially during drives when the guns have to wait, so do not forget a scarf, gloves or an extra jersey or jacket. Many find they have to wear mittens which leave the fingers free if they are shooting. Spectators wear similar clothes when they go beagling.

BARBECUE

Anything goes or almost. Dress to keep warm as the colder evening falls. It is sad, if because you did not bring a hat or scarf, you have to go inside early. In summer open shirts are grand and the cravat for those who wish something other than a tie. The ladies will dress as brightly or warmly as they like.

15

GOING ABOUT AND AROUND

TRAIN JOURNEYS

Cosy compartments for eight people with a corridor for long journeys have been replaced in Britain by open carriages where people sit two facing two on one side and three by three on the other, or in other combinations. There are etiquette guides. If you board a train at, say, Aberdeen and find a reservation ticket pinned to the seat, which shows that the person is not getting on until Edinburgh it would be in order to sit in that seat until Edinburgh. Don't fall asleep hiding the ticket with your head so that he cannot find his seat. That would be bad taste!

Whether to attempt to talk to others in the compartment needs consideration. It is in order to enter the carriage with a bright "good morning" to everybody unless one is young and the others old. Here, in theory, the older ought to acknowledge the younger person first, based on the respect for age theory. Normally, with someone joining a carriage a cheerful "good afternoon" or whatever, is appropriate, creating a friendly atmosphere. Be careful not to start by boring and end by driving someone mad.

A journey I remember was when someone entered the train at Leeds and bored me to death with fishing stories. By the time he had mastered a ram he had hooked when casting behind with a fine line and played it to a standstill, I was bored *because* I did not believe it – a ram being extremely strong would have snapped his line. One has to play these things by ear in train or coach. People around will often be delighted to listen to subjects you raise provided they are light, interesting and not too much about the weather. Avoid too limited topics and back pedal if any of your listeners are f. lling sleep. That may be the time to lapse into silence.

Do not be a crank. On one journey a fresh-air fiend entered the train. It was snowing and this man flung open the window and as the train had built up speed, imagine what happened to his opposite number sitting facing the engine asleep. In seconds the chap was covered in two inches of snow. I will not repeat what he said but I have never seen anybody pull a window up so quickly. Unfortunately the crank immediately lowered it and after several ups and downs the sad story is that the "snowman" had to move to another seat.

One thing not done is to smoke a cheroot, blowing smoke into the eyes, etc., of the passengers. Then there are children with ice-creams. Trains occasionally lurch and kiddies not well balanced are liable to land with their ice-cream in somebody's lap. Parents should control their infants.

So far as trains go, and nowadays they don't always, I have had many interesting conversations and made new friends.

I am reminded of one of our aristocrats who, as the train passed through a station, liked the look of a girl on the platform and pulled the communication cord. He paid the fine but later married the girl. Nor can I forget the time when we were approaching the long Queen Street Glasgow tunnel and my fellow passengers were a pretty young woman and an older man who I took to be her lover. The restaurant attendant just before the train started, had asked if they wanted something to drink. The attractive girl declined politely but the man ordered a double whisky. As the train entered the tunnel it was delivered to him and placed on the table. A moment later, in the darkness of the tunnel, suddenly the lights came on and it was embarrassing for the girl who at that second was having a swig at the man's whisky! Everyone else in the carriage laughed, so beware what you do in tunnels!

RESTAURANTS

No matter what's done in Germany or Texas, in Britain never grab the bell and ring for the waiter, even though there may be a bell on the table. This is an unwritten law. The Englishman with his legendary good taste would never dream of making himself so conspicuous. You show restraint until the waiter hovers near you when you say "Waiter, please", no well-bred person shouts "Hey you".

In theory, guests should order their meals via their host but in practice the waiter usually hovers near each guest and takes their order direct. Far wiser, because the diner can give any special instructions, e.g. "not much fat" or enquire of the waiter about any item he is not clear on.

While no one expects diners to allow themselves to be bullied by waiters it is good taste to avoid too much fuss. This creates discomfort for the other guests who were relaxing. I remember once where closing time was 10.30 p.m. and because one of our companions had not quite finished his biscuits and cheese when the staff began to fidget for people to leave, a man in our group called for the manager. A row developed with threats of writing to the chairman, etc. This is bad etiquette and, in what I call, for want of a better term, the best circles, would not be indulged in. With all our faults and frightening recent deterioration in manners, compared to most countries, Britain is still the finest place to live in. The percentage of kind, nice, honest people is I am sure high here.

ETIQUETTE IN YOUR NEIGHBOURHOOD

Courtesy and good manners can bring enormous pleasure in home or neighbourhood. At the longest, life is short and to develop a good way of living with people is essential to happiness. The few small ways which make it all tick are easily forgotten in the heat of some moment or other.

Somebody moves into a district and begins to erect a high wall or decides without much thought to fell trees which have been there a long time, or perhaps they want to build an ugly garage. Before doing such things people should weigh up the situation and reflect on how the neighbours would regard their actions.

It is usually best to go directly to neighbours, chat over any plans and try and carry them with you in whatever developments you intend. The temptation is often to fly into a rage and begin insulting, or worse, letter writing. Often it is better and a sign of strength to yield to secure peace because otherwise there can be lasting bad feeling among the neighbours. Similarly, to be a good neighbour, those living in flats or terraced houses should control their noise level out of consideration for those living adjacent.

Many of us are bunged up with pride, wrongly imagining it is weak to give in. This doesn't mean that one should be bullied by some nasty neighbour but it does mean consideration for others and a tendency where possible to come down on the side of happy relationships rather than the reverse.

Often a compromise is all that is necessary but there is no doubt if one puts oneself in one's neighbour's place and remembers to "do unto others as you would have others do unto you", then all may be well. For example, one might want to build a garage and the only suitable place for it is near the neighbour's house. Perhaps the problem can be overcome by planting fast growing laurels to camouflage the eye-sore.

WIND PASSING (BELCHING, ETC.)

This comes in two varieties, the voluntary and involuntary. The former in same-sex company, out of doors, is just about acceptable especially for example the belch while lying on the beach following a sumptuous picnic – indeed some regard it as a compliment to the cook!

The involuntary variety can be a little disaster, like losing your dentures on a tennis court. The only hope is to make light of it, apologise and if possible, join in any laughter. What must never be done is to look at someone else – unless that "someone" is a dog.

PICNICS

If you are in the country for a picnic it is ill-mannered to drive your car alongside another picnicker's car if there is other space, yet people do and even blare transistors, sure signs of a poor upbringing. I remember going to Ascot with my friend John Ruffe-Williams and his wife. We were the first arrivals and stopped beneath a tree in the enormous car park (I think it must be twelve acres). While we were laying out our lunch we saw an American car circling around and as the chap appeared to be coming quite close to us, I said to my friends, "that fool's going to hit us". The incredible happened: the man backed into our car, but I will say this for him. He immediately jumped out explaining that he had not realised how close he was and gave us his card. He paid all the cost of the damage. An extreme but good illustration of the wisdom of keeping one's distance from people having picnics.

LITTER AND NOISE

We have a bad name for leaving litter and our kids for making an unholy din when by the sea, especially with loud transistor radios. More recently car radios have become a public nuisance. Experience abroad, confirms we are now worse than other countries certainly so far as litter goes.

IN THE THEATRE

Even if your wife has the most beautiful ostrich feather in her hat, persuade her not to wear it to the theatre. This is extreme but certain women go to theatres wearing big wigs or turn-up collars and such people seem to move a lot so the poor spectator behind has to dodge around to see the play. Do think of others for their pleasure costs just as much as yours. Similarly thoughtless people put up umbrellas at a sports meeting.

We come back to the gravamen of etiquette, namely, THINK OF OTHERS. Be proud of doing that.

PUBLIC HOUSES AND STANDING ANOTHER ROUND

A great English tradition is the pub or inn. It is the meeting place of the kindred spirit, and "lounge" of the stranger far from home.

Introductions are not expected because by custom friendly greetings are passed with acquaintances or visitors. The pub has its disadvantages, especially when it becomes a habit and I am sure many divorces arise because some men go to the "boozer" seven nights a week. Like much in life, pubs have their uses which should not be abused. In some areas or at certain pubs, single females are discouraged – but in most pubs especially if food is eaten, unaccompanied women are welcomed.

Perhaps the worst feature of pubs is what is known as "standing a round". This is a brilliant idea – for the brewers, distillers and wine makers, for in a subtle way, round standing is looked upon as the done thing.

How many have become addicted drunkards because they felt they had "to stand their round" after several others had done so, I do not know. This I know: shy, sensitive people can be embarrassed by feeling they must offer drinks to their groups and it takes courage to say "I will have a soft drink please" or "I've had enough". As an alternative, groups may be formed, one of whose members pays for the drinks and collects a share from each later on or a kitty can be arranged beforehand from which one of the party pays. More people I am happy to report are cutting down alcohol which while fairly harmless if fattening in small quantities is poisonous in excess.

The breathalyser has made excessive drinking and driving a grave matter. The almost impossible to cure alcoholism, is spreading perhaps especially in the middle classes. Well-bred people are slowly changing and there is an increase in soft drinks in pubs, at home or parties. This is good. Even if the breathalyser has done little else, it may perhaps be credited with this. As mentioned elsewhere on smoking the middle and upper classes have all but stopped, and now the movement against intoxication is starting. It has far to go, but good manners demand change, especially in consideration for the families of alcoholics. Excessive drinking at a party is greedy but worse, it is rudeness personified – evil etiquette.

The old attitude must change. If someone refused a beer and asked for a coke, or lemonade the tendency was to sneer. Well-bred people never sneer. They should nowadays counter anyone who does by defending the soft-drinker, whose drink is not habit forming.

THE LONG STARE

Now and then one meets someone or sees someone who stares whether speaking to you or not, that second too long. It is bad manners. Break the habit if you have it.

SNEEZE AND COUGH AWAY FROM PEOPLE

Since it became a fashion for many not to wear suits they don't always have a hanky handy as there are no pockets in many jerseys. If you sneeze at least put your hand up, *turn away* from anyone nearby and apologise. Many who ought to know better, don't do so.

SMOKING ETIQUETTE

Excess smoking connects with etiquette because lung cancer, heart disease, etc, can result from it which in turn means tragedy for relations. Consideration for others means controlling smoking. This killer drug would not be legal had its destructiveness been realised when the "weed" was discovered. As an ex-addict, in the sixty cigarettes a day range, I find it sad that the bad side of smoking so outweighs the undoubted good side. I stopped when I lost the sight of an eye and the specialist warned I would die soon if I did not give up.

The withdrawal symptoms were a nuisance only for days and I am sure those who want to stop ought to make a complete break and suffer the agony of having to chew gum or eat sweets for a few days until the craving passes, as it will, completely. Fortunately price is a deterrent. Indeed, if some people could afford it, they would smoke themselves to death more quickly.

There are tricks which may limit smoking, for instance never before 6 p.m., never before midday and so on but these are more easily written out than carried out. In the modern smaller roomed house it can be inconsiderate to puff away especially if the windows are shut. Smoking in the office is one of the worst offences now so many offices are "open plan" and a compromise could be made by perhaps limiting smoking to certain hours for there is no question that non-smokers can suffer. Among the more intelligent and educated, smoking is declining so rapidly that in many a group of twenty or thirty, no one can provide a light.

WITH THE LADIES

If you have to climb into an attic, even if your lady companion is wearing tights, the polite male goes first, saying "follow me" rather than "after you", and always comes down last.

Another time for care is, if a man is visiting a woman unknown to him, and vice versa. One risk, real enough although rare is blackmail; less common is to find oneself in the home of a sex-nut. This happened to a man friend of mine and was awkward to put it mildly. He found the woman in what looked like a dress but it was split all the way up! Keep a sense of proportion however, for nymphos or their male equivalents are met only rarely.

Most women like to be fussed over if out with you; in a restaurant pull back her chair; if her collar is askew, offer to straighten it; help her on or off with her coat or shoes. In our rush-through life a little old world courtesy is a lovely thing.

GIFTS, TIPS AND PAYING YOUR SHARE

Way back, people who worked for restaurants, railways, hotels, cruise liners, etc. were poorly paid but made up for that by getting tips or gratuities. This being part of their living was understood by the customers and the custom was to tip about 10% of the bill. Tipping generally was more important then though some of the

Unostentatious tipping.

guards on long distance sleeper trains and doormen in a number of London hotels made undue fortunes from tips. Certain renowned hotels *charged* their porters thousands a year to be allowed to work for them! Some of this has died out, but much survives.

Certain nationals are known as good tippers, for example the Americans, while other peoples are considered mean or non-tippers. Unfortunately, tipping is, and perhaps in the future will remain, a "class" thing. I wish it no longer existed but as it does guidance is necessary. One idea of tipping was to reward good service and for those who still tip the quality of service should count. Hotel porters in cities are probably the last stronghold of the big tip and the question arises what one should do. If a porter has carried a lot of luggage for you into the hotel then one would give him a tip.

It is difficult to put a figure on the amount because in expensive hotels the amount would be larger than the cheaper ones. Instead of thinking whether a tip should be £x or £y it is easier to imagine it as giving the man something for a drink. Let's put it this way. For a small service in an inexpensive hotel the tip might be equivalent to a beer but in a luxury hotel the equivalent of a bottle of reasonable wine or even the value of a bottle of gin might change hands for a larger service. Tipping is never done ostentatiously but slightly secretly perhaps deriving from the slang name of a bribe or back-hander! Watch out for the % adding hotel! Ask discreetly at reception if gratuities are included, to save tipping twice.

Taxi drivers are notorious for expecting tips although nowadays some do not tip them. What does happen on a short journey is, if the change comes in round figures to 10% or 15%, people hand the sum in pounds remarking "keep the change". With money values altering even here you would have to give the price of a beer or 10% otherwise one runs the risk of having a hand held out and the question "wot's this?".

Tipping on Cruise Liners

If you buy a drink at the bar or if a steward serves your table you would usually tip him something under 10% of the bill. For example if the change came to say about 5% or 7% you could say "keep the change".

One normally only tips the cabin steward and the table steward at the end of the voyage. The tip would vary greatly depending on how good the service. One uses discretion and the amount following a fortnight's cruise would probably equal the cost of a bottle of whisky for the table steward. The cabin attendant would get half of that. If there is a head steward he might be given a tip, if he has been helpful: luggage porters at the dock side should be rewarded but any tip need not be excessive and depends on the time the porter works for you.

Hairdressers

In some areas they have a box into which tips are put and that saves tearing your hair out! Where the proprietor does your hair it is perhaps unnecessary to tip but otherwise anything around 10% to 12% would be ample, with perhaps a lower percentage where the bill is large.

Gratuities Included (Service Charge)

The continental custom of having the "service charge" included in the bill at either 10% or sometimes 15% is widespread and no tip is then required. The logic is simple. If it is to be included why add it? Nonetheless there are occasions where people like to leave something extra for superb service or enjoyment.

I dislike the "swank" method of calling the head waiter before a meal and tipping heavily in the hope of better service. So far as hotels, restaurants and the like are concerned I think generally if gratuities are included, no tips, and where they are not, use discretion.

Thus in help-yourself restaurants it might be unusual to leave anything "under the plate" whereas in a restaurant with waiters or waitresses any gratuity left or handed over should be based on roughly 10% in the day, but in the evening, the amount could be 12½% to 15%. In a small café or a self-service food counter tipping is rare but appreciated for helpful attention.

It is bad taste to over-tip as this spoils things for those less able to afford the cost. The rich man can always give to a deserving cause but flaunting wealth for personal aggrandizement is a sign of being nouveau-riche and "no gentleman".

Tips in the Sporting Field

Tipping survives here and one has to think out what to do because situations vary. If somebody lends you his boat obviously the chap who looks after the boats would be unlikely to refuse a small tip but if your friend supplies his chauffeur-boatman and you catch a few salmon, at the end of *the* day of your life, it would not do to undertip. For a wonderful day like that one should give the price of possibly even two bottles of whisky. One has got the salmon, and something to talk about for life.

Similarly if out shooting, the keeper, and these men are often part-time farm workers, ought to be tipped, but how much depends on the result. (Tips are not normally passed to all beaters but if, on a thoroughly wintry day, a few nips of some enjoyable liquid are handed round then the beaters – not any juveniles – can be offered refreshment.) If at the end of the day one has been soaked and the bag is two drenched rabbits and a pigeon the keeper would not expect much but if it has been a great day be generous because these men do, to some extent, depend on it. Their wage is often low – lower than many factory workers. It is often wise to consult the host because some shoots (especially syndicates) have rules on tipping. It is not done for the recipient ever to examine the tip in the presence of others! All concerned must pretend to be ashamed and secretive!

Apart from special occasions tipping anyone who has done you a special service needs thought. Some of the younger generation have abandoned tipping so one could almost say, age comes into it. Others who have been tipping all their lives will continue, but many of the younger people have largely cut out gratuities. The recipient of tips may not like the custom and quite a number of people refuse. The use of discretion can avoid offence.

Hotel and Holiday Tipping

In some hotels, where there may be no in-built service charge, you can ask the management to add 10% or a little less to your bill and have it distributed to the staff, or you can deal with the matter yourself – there are usually three people to look after.

a) The porter who helps unload your car or to see you off would get a smallish tip.

b) The maid who does your room(s) who would receive a larger tip, and

c) The head waiter but you should ask him to distribute what you give among all the restaurant staff. This is so that he will know you are not tipping the individual waiters or waitresses.

If you are mainly looked after by one person and don't have much to do with the head waiter, you would tip only your waiter. If you have been well looked after don't hesitate to express your thanks for this means a lot but is rarely done. A message sent to or written on the menu for the chef is kind and will be appreciated.

In the old days in hotels one would estimate 10% of the total bill, dividing that among the three recipients, say 10% of the tip to the porter and 15% of it to the room maid and the balance to the dining room staff but these days as VAT, higher overheads, etc. are included, and tipping is less in fashion, the total is probably based on perhaps 5% or $7\frac{1}{2}$%. It is a personal matter and depends on the situation, e.g. second rate service should receive less, even nothing. Most of us wish the problem would go away.

TAKING A GIRL OUT

A man taking out a girl will not usually find himself expected to pay everything although he may prefer to do so and depending on the situation, a few may insist on it. The modern girl, especially if she is earning, usually prefers paying her share or contributing. A happy arrangement.

One wonders, if, when the idea of sex equality in everything was first mooted, the ladies realised they might have to pay for it! In such matters as cost sharing the equality idea works better than in most areas of life, for as we all know, the sexes are so different and long may it so remain, say some of us.

PAYING YOUR SHARE

Paying your share has become an increasing social custom; once, if a man and wife took friends out to a meal the inviting couple usually paid. When a man entertained a girl he invariably paid (even if he could hardly afford it) but for many years this has changed and what is known as the Dutch method is used. Nowadays couples who arrange to go to a dinner and theatre with neighbours more often agree to "go Dutch". The bill is divided equally by the number present but paid by the men chipping into a kitty as follows: A man on his own need only pay for himself; those accompanied pay two shares – then if a girlfriend wishes to contribute this can be a private arrangement; the couple need not be embarrassed by others being made aware.

In these matters it is exceptionally bad taste to squabble about detail. If you join the group you pay your share(s) as divided by the total number present; you don't claim to have eaten cheaper items off the menu or not to have drunk wine, etc. (although it is polite to suggest a reduction for *others* where appropriate).

CHARITY FUNCTIONS

Some charities would probably be in a mess if they were run on the old basis of collecting money; now something – for example a ball or a whist drive – is staged in exchange for the gift. "Going Dutch" particularly suits such functions.

FLAT SHARING

Paradoxically, in a world where broken homes are increasing, there is a longing to have a place of one's own. This is a development among the young, and where of old several girls or men might share flats, today the sexes are often mixed. Thus a man might share with two girls or three girls or two men with one girl. It's all O.K. so long as the sexes retain separate bedrooms; the rest of the house or flat can be entirely shared, allowing more of a home atmosphere.

An important feature of this development, which takes the place of the old landlady digs, is that those participating should have some mental preparation and have in their minds exactly what they are aiming for, if problems are to be avoided.

Consideration for the flatmates should play an important part. Certain rules should be followed if quarrels are to be avoided. Every arrangement will differ somewhat, but probably most people desire their own privacy and apart from say breakfast, want to attend to their own meals and usually make separate arrangements for entertaining friends.

As a rule, sex plays no part and this should be understood. If the house is to be happy, relationships should be kept platonic unless – and there are always the exceptions – two people fall in love. Flat sharers should realise that if emotional problems are to be avoided this is easier if each keeps out of the other's pocket. To regard it as a money-saving arrangement enabling people to live nearer their work, and to succeed, calls for commonsense and co-operation. It is in sharing that good manners play their part and care in selecting the other inhabitants is essential.

Strict care should be taken of costs (records kept, etc.) such as electricity, telephone, etc. As with all financial obligations of such a personal nature if those who owe (e.g. for rent or telephone) *offer* to pay before having to be asked the person taking the financial responsibility is saved much worry – many people find having to nudge for money distasteful and an unnecessary strain to have to keep thinking about.

Washing up should never be left for others (an odd coffee cup becomes a pile in no time, building resentment too). All should take their share of cleaning and tidying as necessary. Do your bit and keep the home happy!

It is all rather like running a team and if consideration is not shown there can be a disaster.

Due to laws regarding landlords'/tenants' rights anyone sharing or letting part of a flat ought to consult a solicitor.

16
SPORT AND RECREATION

It is easy to go through life frightened of doing something wrong, that is, afraid of putting our foot in it, or to unrealistically imagine that others are all well-bred (better than ourselves anyway) when they are not. In Scotland there is a saying "we're a' Jock Thomson's bairns". Translated this means we are all humans and somebody's children. There may be some who are not quite certain whose children they are and this applies in what used to be called the best circles. Not all Royal children knew who was their dad! So do not worry about whether or not you are as good as another even if, like one Prime Minister of Britain, you may have been conceived on "the wrong side of the blanket".

Equally do not go through life trying to prove you are better than others. A well-bred person neither flaunts his wealth or breeding; in fact he does the reverse. Although activities may be of a competitive nature, avoid comparisons in sport as in life; these merely beget sadness or the near opposite, arrogance. A differing level of skill at something doesn't alter all of us being equal to our fellows as human beings, each one neither better nor worse than another.

DANCING

Not so long ago at big dances guests were given a "programme", a small folded card with a dozen ruled lines, headed first dance, second dance and so on and one had to get the programme filled up. In those days, the man asked the lady to dance with some such expression as "may I have the pleasure of this dance?" to which she had every right to refuse but rarely did. The host checked to see that everyone was getting dances. Such formalities are unheard of today (except for certain special dances where numbers have to be matched). At many balls, dinner dances, etc. there is happily still much old world courtesy. The man nowadays approaches a lady with a "would you like to dance?" or more simply "Dance?" and courtesy demands that she complies unless she has a reason for not so doing. There are people who do not dance but how much they miss! It is still worth learning to be able to foxtrot and waltz despite the impression of television that all is now disco.

If at a dance as part of a group, it is customary to dance with the hostess and her daughter(s). At big dances it is not always possible but it is correct etiquette. If you are married or take a partner to a dance the man should have the first and more important the last dance with his lady; to neglect this is bad manners.

Dignified ballroom dances have largely given way to new types of dancing which to some older people appear to resemble a puppet on a string but actually have, when well executed, a discipline and rhythm of high order. Advanced disco dancing and funky music like the twist can be fun far removed from mere gymnastics.

DISCO DANCING: Like puppets on a string – but keeps one fit so long as the noise does not cause deafness.

TENNIS

There is not a lot to say on tennis because one is unlikely to start playing without a friend to explain the rules but we can deal with etiquette, once again largely consideration and commonsense.

In tennis, one has to avoid poaching a shot from your partner's quarter of the court. The brain has to tell the arm or feet what to do quickly and like most things hurriedly done the result can be wrong. If you have started to go for a ball but get in your partner's way or realise that you have poached a shot say "sorry".

It is correct to apologise to one's partner if one misses an easy shot but don't get good manners on the brain. Few things are more off-putting than a partner forever apologising. One can say "sorry partner, I won't worry you with apologies every time I miss". Fortunately tennis, unlike some sports, has not yet become a battle such as we sometimes see in football where it appears as if the game was to hit the man rather than the ball!

In non-competition tennis although hard shots are played in mixed games the man who frequently hits ferocious returns straight at somebody's middle may find that people do not like playing with him. It is important to avoid too much talking if several courts are in play.

The Ball Hoarder

A discourteous habit in tennis is ball hoarding. Usually separate courts play four or six balls and incredibly in Britain, once renowned for sportsmanship, there are people who conceal a ball or two in their pockets leaving a neighbouring court short. This is not done in decent tennis circles. If extra balls accumulate on your court return these to your neighbour – not during play.

When sending balls back to opponents about to serve – return them to server, not higgledy-piggledy, leaving him to walk about picking them up. When your partner serves it is kind to feed balls to him perhaps pocketing one, till he needs it – but don't fuss over this, do it as opportunity affords.

The Tennis Snob (fortunately rare)

It is not only what they say, rather what they do not say which is bad taste. The type who, while playing his or her shots well, never smiles but scowls, so spoiling the game.

Introducing manners in tennis does more for the game than mere rules. A word of praise and a little encouragement can boost confidence more than an hour's tuition. How one cherishes the memory of being drawn to partner a top player who is never sarcastic and always prepared to praise a good shot! How much one learns. In Britain fortunately there are still many who love tennis for the exercise and fun, more than for the winning.

Thank the Other Players

When play is over you thank your opponents, and your partner for the game. After competitions it is polite, not only at Wimbledon, also to thank and to shake hands with the referee and to thank the linesmen. This is a courtesy indicating there are no bad feelings.

Wimbledon

There are various ways of getting tickets to Wimbledon (for non-Debenture-holders) and the best bet is to:

a) Write for an application form on your letter heading in October to the Secretary, The All England Lawn Tennis and Croquet Club, P.O. Box No. 98, Wimbledon, London, S W19 5AE. You should enclose a self-addressed envelope and if you are writing from U.K. you would put a stamp on it but if from abroad include international reply coupons. When you receive the form, fill it in and return it to the Club before the end of January. The tickets are allocated by public ballot and you will hear from Wimbledon, if you have been lucky, by the end of February when you must send your remittance for the tickets.

b) During the first nine days of Wimbledon, if you arrive early there may well be hope of getting in but after that it is somewhat useless queueing.

c) Another way of getting into Wimbledon is by arriving late in the evening, after 5.30 p.m. People leaving hand back their tickets to the authorities and you can buy these tickets at the gate, if any are available, at a reduced price.

d) Inevitably tickets get into the hands of touts – chaps who will then sell them at the market price! Depending who are the main players, prices vary and one hears of huge sums being paid. So one could say only the rich can use this final hope of getting into the courts.

GOLF – FORE

As in tennis, golf requires lessons even if only from Uncle Bill. One must be careful not to transgress by playing off the tee before the people in front are out of range of being hit. If your ball is going towards another person the rule is you must shout FORE, and beginners should prepare their minds to call the warning out *quickly* and *loudly*. There is the story of the lady of 97 who when asked to what she attributed her longevity replied "by flinging myself on my face with my hands behind my head whenever I hear the word FORE". People taking up the game, need other hints which experience teaches. When addressing the ball, as it is termed, others must remain silent and not move but more important, do not stand close to the player. Stand well away where the player can see you and well behind the ball so that it can't hit you.

GAMESMANSHIP

Gamesmanship is a modern word and not one of which we should be proud. It is mostly indulged in for fun but be careful that the fun does not go beyond a joke! Frequently gamesmanship may do more harm to those who use it than to those against whom it is used. The British tradition of sportsmanship is unique and part of our heritage which we should strive to restore.

There are many great sportsmen and women around the world today who behave well and are good ambassadors for their sports: Sebastian Coe, Tessa Sanderson, Chris Lloyd and Frank Bruno to name but a few.

Sadly, however, it is the badly behaved stars who receive most of the media attention, John McEnroe being a well-known example. It is arguable whether McEnroe would be a better player if he exerted more control over his temper and stopped himself from becoming embroiled in those heated exchanges with tennis officials, but I believe he would. Arguments with umpires reduce one's concentration. The body becomes tense so that regaining relaxation and strength can take time. If an umpire has erred, it usually pays to forget it quickly.

In golf the sportsmanship of professionals and weekenders seems impeccable. It would be for instance unthinkable even if he was unseen, for a player to move his ball to a better lie.

A coin can be tossed for who first plays "off" the first Tee. After that whoever wins the hole has the "honour" to lead subsequently and continues to do so until he loses a hole when your partner leads next time. Only cads miscount their score, yet people have sometimes felt suspicious if a partner says he took 4 to a hole after several four or more letter words coming from behind a bunker!

If playing for money, be sure that the stakes are within your opponent's means; if you are a better player to suggest betting on the result is a little like stealing sweets from babies! Golf has a book of rules which need study but it is the little things, holding the flag so your friend can see where the hole is and helping him to find a lost ball, that make it so pleasurable.

The words "Play the game" are less often heard today which is sad, because while competition has its place, for most it is the companionship, that brings the happy days. Those who take competition too seriously, tend to give up sport too early in life. It is their own loss for, as any top doctor will tell you, as one gets older, more, not less exercise is required.

GOOD CRICKET MANNERS

"It's not cricket, old boy." This is a fitting tribute to a game founded on and steeped in etiquette, tradition and sportsmanship. England has a great heritage in cricket but it has all changed and the days of "The Gentlemen versus the Players" are no more. Sadly, cricket standards, like those of much else except perhaps golf and shooting, have fallen. All the same as my friend the late Major Board once remarked "While cricket is played upon our village greens, the breed of Englishman will remain secure, serene".

The evidence that etiquette still exists is seen in the fact that frequently a batsman will start to walk off the pitch because he knows he had a faint edge or touch to the ball caught by the wicket-keeper or slips. This makes life easy for the umpire as for the fielders. The players all dress in white and none would dream otherwise. The tradition of the hand clap for the good shot or wicket taken is still the custom although sadly in some of the county games its place has been taken in bad taste by clanking beer cans and intoxicated noises so loud that the "wag" or jester in the crowd who interjected and who meant much to cricket is drowned by noise.

Temperament, as in many sports, is still occasionally seen with bowlers kicking down wickets but on the whole the umpires are listened to and obeyed. Many of the bad manners seen today in sport are probably put on largely for the benefit of television viewers now that there are enormous financial rewards.

The climate in sport at last appears to be changing towards sportsmanship, replacing the gamesmanship of recent years and it is a good thing for it would be a sad day for Britain if the words "It's not cricket" lost their meaning. They are part of our language and of our greatness.

HENLEY ROYAL REGATTA

This most English and exclusive Regatta is held on the Henley reach of the River Thames. Competitions are held here in early July and men, and for the last few years ladies, come from any lands to race. Royal Henley is one of the highlights of the English scene.

It is not easy to get into the Stewards Enclosure unless you have rowed for a British University or are invited. If you know a member or anyone belonging to the Leander or other clubs, he might be able to find a place for you. The Stewards Enclosure is a little like Royal Ascot. The ladies dress up and the world's top rowing people enjoy a uniquely British get together, with superb food, drinks and English strawberries and cream.

There is a public enclosure to watch these few days of racing. Entry cost is reasonable but one may have to queue, so it is wise to arrive early.

SOME HORSE RACING MANNERS

Racing has many old and wonderful traditions and numerous lovely racecourses abound in Britain, especially near London. One requires no special dress today for the *non-royal* Ascot, Sandown, York or other meetings although at the Derby and the Oaks (both run at Epsom) a number of men in the enclosures dress in morning suits and their ladies accordingly.

The unwritten rule of British racing is never cheat your bookmaker. Men may mislead their banks, but if you lose, even although in Law you may not have to pay a gambling debt, you must do so.

If you live long enough it is likely some bank manager will mislead you, but unlikely any of Britain's leading bookies will let you down. There is not much fraud in the racing world where one's word is one's bond and people who imagine there is, are I fear, mostly those who back poor horses! If one's horse comes fourth one is apt to think it was a fix, whereas those whose animals win, believe it's all straight. I'm sure no more cheating exists than in other professions or trades.

At many racecourses children are guests and, as they pay nothing, should not be allowed to occupy any seats around the paddock.

No dogs should be taken near a course – although one sees them on the lead at point to points – for they can cause accidents.

BETTING

Beginners sometimes have luck but usually lose. They often go for place bets feeling this is safer than for a win bet but the Tote frequently pays badly for places, sometimes only 11p per 10p bet. The Tote has a minimum stake, but if one uses Tote credit for which you have to open an account, each-way bets can be placed at starting price and smaller sums can be risked. Not all race-goers know that on many courses there is also a betting shop at which an each-way bet can be placed, and this, if the odds for the horse are over 8 to 1, does give a decent place return if there are eight or more runners. In six or seven horse races, only the first two normally count for a place but in some races and in large handicaps place payments are on the first four. If five or fewer horses race it is winner only. One can also bet starting price at the Tote credit windows. Forecasts are fun if you win.

POINT TO POINTS

In olden times men raced each other from one church steeple to another, maybe two miles distant, for a woman's hand or maybe a bet, hence the names, steeplechasing and point to point.

They are popular throughout the British countryside. They provide a wonderful day out for parents and children which need not be expensive, the entrance fee for the car may be the chief cost.

Cars line the racecourse and the day gives an opportunity for mum to provide a lunch hamper for the family.

Between races spectators meander around the paddock and fields meeting members of the hunt, farmers, shooting men, horse lovers, farm workers, woodsmen and all who are part of the local community. It is a typically British social event unlike any other. Overseas visitors love to see this thrilling feature of our way of life.

SHOOTING

Shooting has changed. The days when the gamekeeper taught the laird or farmer's son to shoot are gone although there is another side to it. Then youngsters were thoroughly trained and it was unlikely you would ever find yourself looking down the barrel, or being peppered by a "nouveau riche" gun. It may be only in England that people are referred to as "guns". One doesn't call a tennis player a racquet! I like the expression but guns are dangerous weapons and everyone invited to a shoot should remember the saying:

"Never, never let your gun
pointed be at anyone
that it may not loaded be
matters not the least to me."

Shooting accidents are increasing since the days when shoots were owned by an individual who invited his friends or the shooting was retained by the farmer who chose with whom he would shoot. Accidents appear to have risen in proportion to the increase in syndicate shooting. City men and many business people from overseas often only half taught form a large proportion of today's guns. Syndicates of perhaps 6-12 or more people are the modern method of sharing the cost which has become exorbitant for most individuals.

From "Gun Safety First" (Wildlife Association of Great Britain) by kind permission of the artist.

Many guns have little experience of a sport which should be learned under strict supervision while one is young. This is not the place to go into the subject of safety but suffice to say that a small booklet called "Gun Safety First", is available from The Wildfowl Association of Great Britain.

One safety measure should be stressed – if there is a wounded bird, known as a "runner", it must not be run after. Moving out of either the line of standing guns or if walking, moving out of the line, is one of the ways most guaranteed to get shot! (The dogs will find any wounded bird. Normally a wound is painless during the first hours and few wounded birds fail to be picked up.)

"Poaching"

One etiquette rule is you don't poach another gun's bird or game intentionally. You shoot only at game coming towards you, not if it is approaching the next gun. It can happen by mistake, then one apologises. Standing guns on grouse moor butts are usually placed sufficiently apart to prevent this happening often but it does occur, especially with a curling or crossing bird. It is when some ill-mannered individual does it deliberately that people are annoyed. For correct clothing see Chapter 14.

FISHING

Once again, etiquette stems from kindness. If you see someone fishing from a boat you do not row yours to ten feet from his and start fishing. You keep clear so as not to disturb his "water". Similarly, if you are operating from a river bank you avoid being too close to anyone and, never cut in front of another angler without asking permission.

If two fishermen meet on the bankside, one a fly-rod enthusiast and the other with spinning rod and tackle, the fly angler should be allowed to fish that particular place first. A spinning bait disturbs the water too much for the fly-fisher to follow. This unwritten law arose with the advent of spinning many years ago. Of course the spin-fishing angler can always move on to another likely looking spot, then he can fish the water the fly man has gone over. Fly-fishing does not spoil a water for the spinner.

It might be added that stories of an enormous fish that got away seem to be allowed and it would not be good manners to question too closely the man who is telling you about the 12 lb. trout which broke his line.

MOTORING

The etiquette side of motoring is important because once you remove courtesy and consideration from our roads you increase the number of accidents. Most people if they knew the unwritten code of the highway, would be proud to follow it.

Don't be a Road Dog

People do horrible things with cars, sometimes thoughtlessly, often deliberately, even in anger, hoping they won't be caught or hurt.

Consideration for others includes not turning in people's driveways which wears them out. Also vehicles block entrances, drivers thinking, "I'll be back in a couple of minutes", but then discover a queue at the Post Office counter and as a result some poor soul cannot get out of his own house! It should not be necessary to warn against parking in narrow roads and lanes because of the danger.

No words can describe those cads who through laziness park on both sides of a narrow street or double park making it difficult for others to get through and hazardous for ambulances, fire engines, etc.

Admittedly pedestrians should keep off the roads except at proper crossing places but the modern habit of accelerating and hooting is foreign and terrible.

At the risk of being considered old, I can remember when we had courtesy on the roads and almost everyone was polite. If there was an accident in a car park, a calling card was left under the hand operated windscreen wiper. No-one well-bred was found racing other cars, rather was it de rigeur always to show patience, never temper. It is tempting to be angry, especially at those who will not let you pass. Certainly you would never risk the lives of others in endeavouring to "teach the blighter a lesson". If our modern "road dogs" could realise what pleasure and enjoyment motoring could be, they might well change their ways. Bad manners spoil driving for those guilty of them as well as for the rest. Generally they don't arise because people are in a hurry but because of selfishness or immaturity.

We should develop pride in our driving and show an example which others may follow. Anyone of any social standing does not throw litter out of his car or leave it lying about after picnics, etc.

Thumb a Lift

It is a risk to give anyone a lift who thumbs one, whereas if they don't, it should be safe. Years ago the custom was to pick up almost anyone but recently so many have taken advantage of this kind act, that it is not a good idea. Sadly in our age where it is unsafe to walk about at night, giving any lifts has to be undertaken with care.

If I was travelling in the country and noticed someone waiting for a bus or walking in a lane, depending on the weather and what they looked like, age, etc. I might stop and offer a lift. Many however will refuse, because they in turn, are afraid which is a sad reflection on our time. The best advice is against giving lifts especially at night. The same thing applies to helping someone whose car appears to be broken down. It could be genuine but might be a trick so be cautious.

YACHTING

If you are invited to go on a yacht several points should be considered. You should take the correct sea-going clothing and footwear, and learn a few technical words about a boat. Try to gather as much knowledge as you can in advance especially about safety afloat. This will simplify things for the captain as well as for you. Do *not* ignore the possibility you may feel sick! It is not only a courtesy to try and prevent this, it is a matter of safety, not just of yourself, but for the other crew. Should a small boat find itself in difficulties, a sick sailor can be a major hazard. Do not rely on the yacht having tablets on board. Have some of your own. It is wise to experiment with tablets at home because some types may induce drowsiness. Remember all types need to be started an hour or so before setting sail. One way to reduce sickness liability is to keep busy. A supervised turn at the tiller (or wheel) is excellent if your skipper agrees, but at worst you may have to go below and lie down.

There are various types of yacht – they may specially suit the area of their home base, e.g. south coast or east coast, being adapted for the sort of cruising found around there or perhaps purpose built for racing, however you would be unlikely to be invited to join a racing yacht first time out.

Clothing Ashore

Back in the yacht club "south coast" people used to be more "regulation" – blazers and flannels – minded, where in other areas smart jeans, and something such as a Guernsey sweater were accepted. Nowadays more casual attire is the form all round but when some special event like a regatta is on, expect people to be more formal. Ask your host beforehand if any such event will arise. A considerate captain will generally raise the subject of clothing at the time of the invitation anyway, but can be forgiven if he should forget because planning a passage on a yacht, even for a weekend, is quite an undertaking without having to think of everything for the crew to wear as well.

Despite today's informal atmosphere a general yachting maxim remains that on land at least, the dress of gentlemen sailors of both sexes (bearing in mind the occasion) should never be "aggressively scruffy". The problem of taking a lot of clothes, such as a dinner jacket for a dance however is that of stowing them in the small locker space available. You therefore find that gentlemen can wear a blazer (with tie or cravat) and flannels and the ladies a dress or skirt for all but the most formal evening ashore.

Clothing Afloat

Shoes are important because wet decks are slippery. The safe wear is a non-slip rubber soled sailing shoe, or better still sailing boots; a tennis-type shoe will not be accepted by the more seamanlike skipper. High heels would damage a deck and smooth soles could slip you overboard. Be sure you have or borrow "oilies". These tops and bottoms not only exclude water; they keep cold winds out and help prevent you getting perished. Jeans and *plenty* of sweaters are fine for underneath. A towel round your neck prevents water sluicing down. A minimum of one complete change of clothing is necessary because if rough conditions blow up you may still be soaked through at some stage. To have nothing dry available would be foolhardy and because of the cold possibly dangerous. Do not rely on good weather or selfishly being able to borrow from others. Have a swim suit too. All should be packed in a bag, preferably waterproof, which can be rolled into a ball to store.

If you are a non-swimmer do tell your host at the outset. He will want to take special steps such as issuing a safety harness early on if the sea looks like getting lumpy or if you appear sickly.

Which Side Shall I Sit?

One episode which happened, contained a subtle issue of etiquette. I emerged up the companionway in a heavy sea and yelled through the roar of the lashing waves to the captain "which side shall I be sick?". He thought I shouted "which side shall I sit?" and pointed to the windward side (on which in normal health you would sit) instead of the correct side (to be sick over) the leeward side when the wind is of course behind you.

Nautical Jargon

For the peace of mind of the "regular" crew, a few suitable nautical words should be learnt, and not those of the "shiver me timbers" variety! *Bow* (sharp end), *stern* (blunt end), *mast* (spar sticking up), *boom* (horizontal spar attached to mast), *sheet* (rope controlling end of sail), *halyard* (rope to pull sail up mast); these may be all that are necessary – together with *port* and *starboard.* There is a useful phrase for this last pair: "No more red port left", which has the advantage of reminding you that the red light is carried on the port (left) side at night. (Green light is on the starboard side.) "*Ready about!*" is a warning from the helmsman that he is about to turn into and through the eye of the wind. Those detailed must be ready to man the sheets and adjust the sails for the new direction. "*Gybe Ho!*" (shouted) alerts you to get your head down as the boom is about to lash across, propelled by the wind getting round from one side of the back of the mainsail to the other. "*Man overboard!*" requires instant disciplined reactions and you should make sure you are familiar with your skipper's views on the subject so you would know what is expected of you in this unlikely event *before* any such a mishap occurs.

"Gybe Ho!"

Much of what is said above applies equally to dinghy sailing although we have dealt mainly with cruising in bigger boats. Avoid standing in small boats; always keep the centre of gravity low. There are many more seamanship rules for yachtsmen and small boat sailors to know but generally you need not worry as first-time guest.

Yachting is expensive so if you are invited it is thoughtful to take a contribution to the food or drink department or offer to share some of the cost.

BOWLS

Etiquette here is based on established tradition which sets companionship and concern for others above all, especially as many physically handicapped people play bowls.

Never walk on a green unless wearing bowling shoes which are completely flat, or rubber overshoes which can be hired at most greens.

A bowler should not go onto the mat until the previous bowl has stopped and its position indicated by the Skip.

Players should keep still and quiet and far enough back to avoid shadows in front of the mat when a player is about to bowl. It is considered a serious breach to talk to another person on or off the rink whilst bowling is in progress and an even greater offence to talk to a person on an adjacent rink (thereby obstructing two games).

All players on a rink should assist with the clearing of a head once it has been played and the score recorded. Bowls should be collected and placed behind the mat but *not* immediately behind it (to avoid back-stepping foot traps).

Players in any position must not interfere with their opponents, distract their attention or in any way annoy them. Furthermore, players standing at the head of the green, unless directing play, must stand behind the jack and away from the head. All players at the mat end of the green, other than the one actually delivering a bowl, must stand behind the mat.

Discuss dress with any experienced bowler as players are rather particular on this subject in many clubs.

HUNTING AND RIDING

More etiquette exists in hunting than in any other sport. It has existed for centuries and while people criticise huntsmen, hunting is less cruel than keeping chickens in cages. Foxes kill lambs and if they get amongst chickens or any young birds they bite their heads off and I have found half a dozen headless chickens lying around. In fox hunting, frequently the fox's skill enables it to escape and so it has a good chance. Foxes often reach great age and are prolific breeders. There are other ways of killing foxes, by digging, gassing or snaring, poisoning or trapping but these are more cruel than hunting. Hunting is a feature of the British way of life, giving employment to many.

Hunt Servants

Whippers-in are referred to as servants. They have to be obeyed and one must give way to them and the pack (the hounds). Boxing Day is a great day for hunts and local hound shows. At the end of the season there is usually a Hunt Ball while a dinner is generally given separately for the farmers and other friends of the hunt.

Dress

Hunt coats are referred to as scarlet or pink but one never talks of them as red! For safety, leather boots are considered essential and hunting people tend to frown on anyone using rubber boots. Rightly or wrongly one should try to comply with these customs.

Cubbing (hunting young foxes) dress is a hacking jacket but never a black jacket. Black boots are worn with a black coat but one would not wear black boots with brown edging unless one had a pink or scarlet coat. These finer points show the necessity for anyone riding with the hounds to check the custom for the area of the hunt in which they ride, so as not to offend.

The Master of Hounds (M.O.H.) can wear a velvet cap with ribbons at the back pointing upwards which indicate his status. Spurs are always used as is a hunting whip, to aid the whipper-in, if need be. The M.O.H. carries a long whip which he can crack.

When confronted with a red ribbon on a horse's tail, stand clear. It means a kicker. A green ribbon means a young horse, possibly nervous.

Hunting Words

You refer to hounds as couples (dog and bitch), and at the end of the day the huntsman counts the hounds. If your horse is fit you would say that it is in *good nick*. One does not refer to hounds as dogs, and a terrier, in hunting terms, is used to dig out foxes.

At the Meet

1) A lady bows and says "good morning" to the Master. A man raises his hat and the Master would doff his to any lady follower, as well as returning the simple wish for a good day.

2) Never overtake hounds or cross a line of scent.

3) Do not jump in pairs as one horse could bring the other down. A gentlemen gives the lady a "lead" over jumps unless she wishes to go first.

4) In the field there must be deathly silence, no smoking, perfume or after-shave, etc, because a fox can sense humans quickly.

5) If riding over cultivated or seeded fields keep to the edge no matter where the hounds run. On heavy plough choose a furrow with casual water in it as this ground which holds the water, will usually hold your horse.

6) Riding along a bridle path leave a safe distance between you and the horse in front in case it stops or falls.

7) Children or newcomers open gates keeping well back for the horses to go through and they must be sure to shut them. Children who behave and help the hunt can win hunt buttons from the Master.

8) Damage to property must be reported to the Master with an offer to pay.

9) Your horse's head must face the hounds, never his hind quarters – or you will be rebuked and if the offence was continued could be "sent home" – the ultimate disgrace!

10) Finally, all good horsemen see their horse is "done up" properly, and fed bran mash before attending to themselves.

General Points

If a fox hunter has some acquaintance with "the music of the chase" he finds greater enjoyment. Without some knowledge he would be regarded as a mere *"galloper"*. For example, hounds respond to certain calls and if the rider understands these, it helps to prepare him for the "off" or "stand still" and "listen". To illustrate: when a hound "winds" a fox in the woods he makes a "wow", the other hounds and huntsmen hear him and the following notes on the horn indicate the situation. You can read a horn like a book if you listen and learn. The horn is used in three ways:–

Tootingly – one toot in the woods means "I am still here"; two toots say "I am turning round"; three toots mean things such as "where is my flask, or sandwiches", or it may mean "bring all hounds over here".

Wailingly – three hoots means "the cover has been drawn and is blank, let's get on to another fox". However, at the end of the day (you will know because you will feel tired) this signal will mean "we are going home".

Trillingly – three toots mean "come on, here is a good fox out in the country. Let's get on to it".

The Horn's Notes

Nearly impossible to set down on paper but one gets to know the sounds which help you to appreciate what hunting is all about. For example, a single note of medium length means the hounds have finished their kill. When it is desired to change the direction while searching for a fox, the hunt would be called by two short blasts. Another example is three short blasts which tell the hunt servants that a fox has been scented.

It gets too complicated to continue in a book of this scope, for example if the hounds are lost and have to be recalled, five longish blasts only slightly connected is the sign given.

Voice Signals

There are other expressions such as "ditch to you" and "ditch from you" meaning that the ditches besides the far off fence or hedge are on one side or the other, but this book is only introductory and before riding to hounds one would have to be guided by experienced riders.

RIDING AND COURTESY ON THE ROADS

Ride in single file close to the hedge or bank on the left side, look back frequently and signal passing traffic when safe to overtake. Signal your own movements as if you were on a bicycle. Keep your horse under control and don't slop along absentmindedly which is dangerous.

Keep to the edges if the field is ploughed or sown, *do* shut gates behind you so that livestock cannot stray. Avoid riding too close to pedestrians which can frighten them and create an anti-horse public. Always say "good morning" to those you meet. Similarly, if you enter a livery yard don't ignore the owners but give them a bright greeting. Many of the instructions for riding to hounds of course apply to ordinary riding.

This popular sport generally requires to be taught professionally. However there are parts of the country far from busy roads where children have ponies or ride those belonging to friends without proper instruction. This is dangerous because horses, particularly young horses or ponies, are strong and can be obstreperous. The horse usually is a highly strung animal and a few minor hints may be useful. Never stand right in front of a horse because they tend not to see you. You stand normally on the horse's left side. By doing this, if the horse rears you are less likely to be "pawed". Dangerous as it can be standing in front of a horse, that is usually as nothing to the danger of standing behind it!

When leading a horse on a road you place yourself on its right so that you are between the horse and the traffic. In the next paragraphs we have been generously allowed to use ideas from the Royal Society for the Prevention of Accidents' pamphlet called "Riding on the Road". These leaflets can be purchased from RoSPA, Cannon House, The Priory Queensway, Birmingham B4 6BS (Tel. 021-233 2461).

If crossing a road, look right, left, and right again before emerging and with a wildish horse it is wiser to lead it than to ride across. If there are several riders together it is better to have them assemble and wait until the road is clear to let the party over. It is risky for some horses to cross leaving a few to follow, as horses like to be together.

When trotting, care must be taken when turning as horses can slip. Traffic and police signals apply equally to riders as does the Highway Code. Where there is a grass verge, unless you are prohibited from doing so, or it is outside a private home, ride on it. One essential of riding is to concentrate because the horse knows if you are not.

On roads or paths it is usual to ride single file and if there are several of you it is best to ride in columns of four or five with a gap of about 100 yards between groups, which will help passing traffic to leap-frog the cavalcade during safe moments. Children or beginners should ride in the middle of a group and never in the lead or last. In suitable conditions it may be wiser if one horse is nervous to ride two abreast keeping the nervous one on the inside.

Twilight Riding

Many children after school stay out riding too long in the twilight. They should wear something white and carry a light showing white at the front, red at the back. These lights can be made to attach to the stirrup. Another idea is to use a strip of reflective material round your ankles. Fluorescent reflective bands or over-jackets are a good idea for night riding and these are obtainable at most good riding-tack or cycle shops.

Hints for Slippery Roads

Dismount. Lead your horse; because he has four legs he is less likely to fall than you. If you insist on riding on a slippery road do "de-stirrup" for safety. For peace of mind do have some form of third party insurance. This shows true consideration. Riders should wear a hard hat for safety.

If riding at the edge of a field or in woods beware of low barbed wire – tripwire – found in some areas to hinder trespassers.

17

ETIQUETTE IN BUSINESS AND AT WORK

England is becoming increasingly like America with numerous conferences, luncheons, business entertainments, etc. There have always been office celebrations for people retiring, Christmas parties and so forth but these have extended into get-togethers for salesmen, market researchers and others who can get in on the action! You name it and there will be a dinner, a weekend – semi-holiday – conference or even a week abroad covering this product launch or that crash course. The mix of business and "pleasure" can prove an uneasy one at best with "friendship" tending to suffer from lack of genuine spontaneity.

The growth of all this is partly due to the tax policy in the last 30 years. Without added inflation such things would probably have remained limited. But as things are, people are apt to seek anything that appears to promise fun while avoiding personal expenditure and tax.

BUSINESS ENTERTAINING

Part of the trouble may be that many can no longer afford to entertain privately. The British, however, are adept at finding ways to enjoy life despite the ravages of monopoly, union power, EEC protectionism and VAT. In place of house parties formerly given, we find these quasi-enjoyable but frequently useless substitutes being sported under the guise of business.

Persons of independent mind attend as few such functions as possible. However, there are arguments in favour and many believe achievements come easier in the happier atmosphere for example by the sea. Giving lectures and meeting men in such surroundings has also been used successfully in the services, where other ranks associate with their officers in a more relaxed atmosphere. It is claimed selection boards are able to choose the best officers in this way.

In civil life, such "*social*" meetings may be for the purpose of attending lectures, demonstrations, etc. but it is regrettable that there may also be an element of reward for unexceptional work merely so that a good time, dancing or visiting places between study periods can be had by all at *taxpayers' expense*.

Hopefully, more often the purpose is genuine, for example, to enable management to get acquainted with those who have not yet been chosen for special tasks, promotion or an overseas job. Good manners therefore assume importance.

AT WORK OR NOT AT WORK?

It is easy to behave at work, but in the happier atmosphere of drinks being served at the conclusion of some conference for instance it is well to know that someone may be noticing your behaviour.

ETIQUETTE STEMS FROM CUSTOM AS WELL AS KINDNESS

One maxim which remains a conventional *wisdom* has reached us from former days via the military services. In the mess no officer or gentleman shall speak of politics, sex or religion. Another *professional* dictum bars discussion of money in polite society.

The impact of legislation upon wealth and freedom, of the pill and free sex discussion, of collapsing religious domination, and of the diminishing value of what money we are allowed to keep has changed all this. Now, in selected or limited doses, these formerly tabooed subjects, are commonly aired. It is now accepted in engaging a doctor, solicitor or chartered accountant to inquire as to the likely fee. Within the flirtatious atmosphere of courting, the sounding out of religious views or oblique reference to the pill are no longer considered to be unmentionables. Today, a political stance, provided it is not laboured (no pun intended) can be taken without offence, although it should not be prolonged enough to bore. If in doubt, ask your listener(s) if you are boring, offering to stop.

After that digression – an important matter to mention is excessive drinking, which often brings out the worst in people. Many promotions have been lost through liquor loosening the tongue. Guests not realising they are on test can make various blunders. Other than too much to drink, beware of such misdemeanours as telling naughty stories in mixed company – what is funny among men, may shock the boss's wife. And avoid making gossip. Steer clear of noisy debates with management if you are interested in advancement but being a mouse when you are convinced you have a valuable contribution to make will *lose* you respect. So beware of dropping your guard or letting your hair down too much, but don't be afraid to say what you think when sure of your ground.

TOO MANY RAT RACES

The term "the rat race" is of recent origin and nowadays businesses are frequently run almost without heart although mostly complying with the law. To give an example: a couple of generations ago most companies were conducted in a friendly way. In the '30s, depressed as things were, there was immense kindness. For instance, businessmen who were strong in capital resources, etc. would frequently allow a competing firm to secure an order, not because they could not compete but because they knew that the other company desperately needed work. During the last war a company was bombed out. Next day, a dozen competitors had offered to help by fulfilling contracts – despite everyone being under staffed. This typified the wonderful spirit that was once Britain. The same spirit, found in all classes, was and is still found in many areas and if capitalism is allowed to function properly, we can hope it will return.

THE CHANGING FACE OF CORRUPTION

From the thirties to the sixties British integrity and high-mindedness stood as high as it had in the first two decades of the century. Across the world an Englishman's word was his bond and he didn't need to "put it in writing". Everyone believed British was best. If it "wasn't cricket" an Englishman didn't do it. Today I regret to have to suggest we have as a nation much deteriorated though ours is probably still the best country to live in.

HISTORY REPEATS ITSELF – DIFFERENTLY

History tends to repeat itself in different ways. As inflation exploded in the seventies and destructive taxation accompanied it, the easy way to get rich was to cheat, steal or take advantage of legal loopholes by tax avoidance. Unfair though usually legal ways to concentrate on capital gains became "acceptable" but more commonly tricks were used to obtain government grants or handouts, without work.

Fringe benefits, manipulating redundancy payments, extra social security money obtained by lies and the like all played their part in damaging our reputation.

The Common Market with its elephant-sized swindles by several countries, notably France and Italy and recently Germany, has set a frightening example of making crime pay. Our once great country has been influenced by the E.E.C. and sadly not for the better. Add our inflation and the new protectionism of the Common Market, both creating dishonest money, and we can see why greed has largely replaced good.

All this has much to do with etiquette for when a nation abandons or loses its moral standards and principles, individuals' consideration for other people is undermined.

If my instinct is correct that inflation is an important reason for the fall in standards and decent manners, then reducing inflation assumes more than political significance. Expense accounts and inflation-related pay or pensions *being only for some*, all increase humbug and class hate which I perceive are greater now than at any time this century.

While our corruption is more subtle than that of the twenties it is interesting to note that as the depression was overcome in the thirties, with returning competition, inflation receded. Competition makes it less possible for whiz kids or crooks to get the money with which to corrupt. We are paying the price in the eighties for the money printing political tricksters of earlier years.

Inflation changes the character of a nation's people. To the detriment of those who humbly toil, the money-lending organisations, the capital gainsters, land and farm owners, the property boys, and others, even house buyers who got in before inflation – all, through no effort, benefit beyond the dreams of avarice. It damages the small or medium capitalist as well as the middle classes and professional families. They who in the past were the upholders of good manners have lost influence and suffered. We can hope all of this will change for the better.

We conquered inflation in the twenties and in the thirties the U.K. led the Western world out of the depression. Our recovery of 5% a year was quicker than that of any other land. It will be interesting to watch if history repeats itself.

DOES HONESTY PAY?

Some sneer at the old saying "honesty is the best policy", but here is a story. A product buyer of an international company employing thousands was so honest he would not accept a cigarette from a visiting salesman. I used to think he was carrying integrity a little far. He was not specially clever, but so great was the trust in him that this man of humble origin and education is now a managing director. His work and honesty paid. *Except in inflationary times,* my observation is that it still does.

BRIBERY OVERSEAS

This is a problem and has always been. British and American politicians seem blind to that. We have heard of slush funds, but in parts of the world the only way large contracts can be obtained is if a number of agents are "taken care of". Even our two-faced political leaders recognised this some years ago by allowing entertaining costs to be charged before tax only for overseas customers. Standards of conduct and morals differ in other lands. Bribery in this context is called introductory commission or agency fees and you either go in for it, or the business goes to other countries. We cannot control the world and it is hopeless to try.

LOOK AFTER GOODWILL

Thank heaven there are still in business millions who do not entirely allow their heads to run their hearts. Firms who look after, not only their profits but their goodwill, both with staff and customers, have much advantage. Marks & Spencers, to give an example, are not world-leaders – selling more per square foot than any store in the world – because they are hard-faced or treat their staff badly. It is the opposite. They were among the first companies to start a staff welfare department. They are said to pay higher salaries than most. Customers can change the goods at any branch if they do not like them. I believe (and it is as nearly proved as most things) that courtesy and fairness not only cost little but pay well. Apart from the happiness that behaving in what might be called a Christian or humanitarian way brings, there are rewards in this world too! Big rewards.

BIG CAN BE UGLY

The obsession for ever bigger business, councils, schools, etc., appears to be changing with the rediscovery that "small is beautiful". Graciousness and good manners come more easily in smaller units. Life where courtesy and consideration are missing is less worth living.

CHRISTMAS TIME STAFF DANCES AND OTHER SIMILAR FUNCTIONS

As some of the younger men might not have a dinner jacket a

considerate management will request lounge suits for them and for the girls afternoon dresses which save embarrassment and expense.

Anyone organising such affairs should make a list of the basic essentials. Even at a firm's party or annual outing, someone should be detailed to see that for example the most junior or new member is catered for and not left to feel isolated. Remember to thank the partners or directors and organisers.

AT WORK BENCH OR OFFICE

A place of work should be like a happy ship or home. The worst type of office bore is the one who goes on about his generation being the wonderful super-duper one. Such people always complain of the old or young who, according to them, are a shower of no-goods. There are good and bad in all age groups. What has happened is that the affluence of recent years has changed the relationships between people, because wealth is more widely spread. We may condemn modern education but there are several good things about it. The young no longer respect the old on account merely of age. An employee does not now feel obliged to bow and scrape lest he be sacked. Ours is an age of rebellion not all of which is bad, but respect should accrue to those who deserve it.

The effect of less discipline in home and education and on television has also much changed the world. Among the benefits it has reduced shyness, and some of today's employers have been forced to become more understanding.

OFFICE OR FACTORY POLITICS

People at work should avoid office politics, scoring off others or sarcasm even if done for fun. Those indulging in what can be called verbal horseplay, should remember that there are people who, although they may not show it, are deeply hurt by derogatory remarks.

RETIREMENT OR LEAVING GIFTS

We should try to be original and the old idea of a speech and a clock can often be improved upon by giving thought and adapting the present to the person concerned. Thoughtfulness is the stuff of which memories are made. Some might find a clock a nuisance for many homes have no mantelpieces today and most of us have watches. A firm might present a beautiful electric trolley or if the company could afford it, what could be nicer than a sea trip for the man and his wife or perhaps even a car for long loyal service.

Recently when a doctor retired from an area after 51 years, a committee was formed and he was given a dinner with 500 guests many of whom travelled hundreds of miles. A clever way of collecting was that in the invitations it mentioned a cheque was to be presented but the limit for any guest was £10. Most gave this amount. A happy event for one who had devoted his life to his patients.

OTHER HINTS

In meetings where discussions are taking place the chairman must try to be fair to everyone. It is important to ensure that all, especially those who might be shy, are encouraged to express their views. It is hard to hear what others are saying whilst you are interrupting!

COURTESY TO VISITORS

Too many people treat business visitors as if they were intruders letting them wait often for an hour which a little rearrangement and consideration could reduce. Courtesy can be profitable even if regarded materialistically. The damage most of us do to ourselves in our business relationships is due to our own behaviour. Put differently, the blows we suffer in life come mostly from an unknown source and conversely much of the profit in business results from goodwill of which one rarely knows the source. In business, etiquette demands that people be treated decently no matter whether they are tea ladies or lord mayors. The sign of a well-bred person is that he behaves to everyone alike. The best opinion of the boss of a firm employing 100 people can usually be had by asking the most junior office boy or girl. No boss can fool his staff for long.

SOME BUSINESS RULES

Many firms have rules about manners and certain courtesies are overlooked for reasons of efficiency, for instance opening doors for ladies or standing up if a girl enters a room. Some firms even cut down on "pleases and thank yous" but this may be going too far. Explain such rules to new staff who should be welcomed and shown cloakroom facilities on arrival.

Never ever should a boss or manager correct or admonish staff in front of others – unless in exceptional circumstances. Leg pulling, a British habit, should not extend to causing pain. We are back to the basics of good taste; think of the other person as much or more than of yourself. It is usually foolish to tell tales against other staff, for you have to work in close proximity and *people do have feelings*

SHOPKEEPERS

Many shopkeepers are polite to customers while treating visiting salesmen without respect. Often if a customer comes in, the shopkeeper will leave the representative to whom he is speaking and go over and attend to the customer. No one minds that, but he should say to the representative "Excuse me for a moment" and show courtesy instead of low breeding.

Once upon a time all assistants were subservient to customers but that has changed. Nonetheless courtesy still gets its reward. Shop staff and all in similar positions will obtain more joy in their work if they co-operate and help people. We think too much of our "rights" and forget there is nothing infra dig in giving top service. The doctor who removes 12 appendices daily, even if highly skilled, is giving a service which, for him, may be boring. Yet all good doctors are unfailingly courteous to their patients. Sadly these days there seem to be fewer good doctors and, alas, fewer courteous patients. Cause and effect?

TRAINING STAFF TO BE COURTEOUS

In competitive business goodwill is vital. It is built up in 100 ways and staff ought to be trained to cultivate it. An example would be to see that a long distance lorry driver was offered a cup of tea on arrival, while a visitor who has come a distance should be offered toilet facilities to "freshen up". Many office staff, including seniors, could learn from most of our well-mannered telephone exchange girls.

CONFIDENCES AND TRADE SECRETS

A good secretary knows that what her boss tells her or what she overhears is secret. That rule is often ignored and staff of various grades, not excluding some directors (usually unintentionally), spill information to friends in pubs and the like. Whether in error or with malice, employees should remember giving away such information is illegal and unfair.

Competitors, in ways unheard of a generation ago, now set traps and try to steal trade secrets, even methods of running a business, from the unwary. They seek information, be it names of suppliers, operating methods or secret manufacturing formulas which may be the result of 50 years of hard work. Exposing or spreading such information is immoral as well as idiotic. Giving away confidential information could cost you your job, or even destroy the company.

STEALING TIME AND WORSE

A generation ago a common expression of Trade Union leaders was to urge "a fair day's work for a fair day's pay". This has rarely been used in the 'eighties. Gradually and regrettably attitudes have altered in the U.K. towards the practice of getting as much money for as little work as possible (less work in the same hours amounts to stealing the employer's time). This "theft" did not occur in U.S.A., Germany or Japan to the same extent, which partly explains Britain's troubles. Nor was theft confined to time. In a number of Britain's shipyards, for instance, stealing was so extensive that companies employing thousands had to close. In airports, etc. today it seems to be a habit. Large helpings to private phone calls and franking of personal mail abound. The increase in theft is a cause of unemployment. Theft hardly embraces consideration for other people! Fair play and honesty by contrast not only have their relevance in etiquette but help to maintain employment.

INSOLENCE TO SUPERIORS

Some young or inexperienced staff may imagine it clever to try insolence on their managers or directors. Under newish legislation such ill-mannered people may be convinced they can get away with such unruliness. A few may but not usually for long. How many careers are jeopardised by a few stupid rebellious words?

STAFF FRIENDSHIPS

Should a person mix with work colleagues or mates? Is it wise to form staff friendships or treat work as different and avoid becoming close to others on the staff?

The answer is that it depends on what you mean. For the ambitious it is probably wise to keep one's social life clear of work but against that there is nothing in the code of manners to prevent developing friendships. In fact, many a boss or professional man has married an employee, or the other way round. Doctors marry nurses, pilots air stewardesses. Great care is needed in such friendships not to cause pain or offence; it is generally wiser to look for romance among outside friends, but rules are sometimes made to be broken.

DEALING WITH BANKERS

Avoidance of quarrels contributes much to the maintenance of good manners and happiness. This "negative" side of etiquette is important, and regrettably often applies to relations with bankers. Bankers have changed – the old time manager is dying out. The gentlemanly ex-public or grammar schoolboy who had your firm's interest at heart has been replaced possibly by his son, who is a child of near bank monopoly and reduced competition.

The big six or eight clearing banks are now down to four thanks to weak governments allowing them to amalgamate. This has reduced competition and increased the bankers' power over businessmen. For good relations with your bank try to have several banks. Thus, if that nice manager is replaced, as happens, by a nasty type, you should be able to change banks. Alas such an ideal spread of your custom is not always possible and one also has to consider if it may be wiser to stay with the branch to establish a longer "track record" for later in your life. Managers are usually changed every few years and bad ones more often!

I believe it unwise for a married couple to have a joint account; indeed it is better to arrange for your wife to bank elsewhere. Banks love the former as it gives them a near stranglehold. I consider it equally foolish for people to give a bank preference over a building society when buying a house which at once increases the bank's influence over you. "Absolute power is absolute evil."

TELEPHONING

There was once an advertisement "If you want to get ahead, get a hat". Everything changes and not many wear hats but we could coin a saying, "If you want to get ahead, get a good telephone manner". Even though we live in an age when the telephone is in daily use, it is astonishing how many people are still unsuccessful with this instrument.

From an etiquette point of view there are plenty of occasions when a telephone can and perhaps should be used but certain other situations where it should not. One needs, for example, to be careful not to be drawn into venting angry feelings on a telephone because of the risk of slander, or more commonly of hurting somebody's feelings.

Quite a few people seem to get flustered about telephoning perhaps because they are unable to see the person at the other end. Since a telephone conversation cannot *hurt* physically – after all, the other person is possibly miles away – the fear may arise in being unprepared or in feeling insecure dealing with what the person at the other end may wish to discuss. Or, faith in one's own melodious tones carrying themselves faithfully over the wire may need to grow – something which happens naturally with practice.

Planning – Put It On Paper

Before starting a telephone conversation do do some planning. Before you ring up have a piece of paper with reminder headings of what you want to talk about. This prevents you having to ring back a second time when you remember things you forgot. Here is an example.

1. Bill/holiday/August?
2. Bill's mother-in-law/whereabouts then.
3. Phone number of Jack's restaurant.
4. Jean/map of Yugoslavia – borrow?

Libel and Slander

Libel exists when something derogatory is written down; even if what is written is true, unfortunately the law of libel can still apply. This is partly because statements are notoriously difficult to prove. It is thus sometimes said, *"The greater the truth, the greater the libel"*. Slander is where something of a libellous nature is *said* rather than written. Do be careful to avoid slandering anyone on the telephone. The receiving end may have an extension with a "witness" listening in. Indeed I'm afraid this method is often used intentionally to collect evidence.

Uses and Abuses

We read in the papers that bugging of conversations takes place but most of us can forget about that. Nevertheless the lesson of being discreet on the 'phone is one well learnt.

The telephone is appropriate to invite people to informal parties or meetings, but special parties need to be carded.

It can also be useful in expressing sympathy particularly where someone might find it difficult to write a letter. But there is more to it. Although we can't all have or develop a newsreader's accent undoubtedly those who use a telephone with confidence, can achieve what an ordinary user may not. As telephone use is likely to grow relative to the slowness of letters we should learn to master it. In the days when the post was reliable and one could count on next day delivery that method was more widely used. However, it can't compare with a telephone conversation. With all today's rush the skilful 'phone call can fortunately restore leisure time enormously.

A nice polite clear voice and confident pronunciation makes an enormous difference to what can be achieved. If the call is planned it saves time and cost. In that regard *always* keep a pencil and paper beside your 'phone.

To increase your practice why not throw out suggestions perhaps at the office or home that you be allowed to take incoming calls? The way to improve one's telephone technique is to gain confidence. Anyone who has employed a top secretary will realise the difference this makes if one is away from home. Instead of finding a message on your desk, "Mr. Wilson called", you find a message like this: "Mr. Wilson of the Die Stamp Company, Aberdeen, telephoned. He wants to know whether he can call on you on 24th November to discuss delivery dates for the new machine? His phone no. is . . . . . ."

Increasing confidence comes through in the voice. Since children can begin handling a 'phone even before schooldays it is rather a pity that our schools don't teach people how to develop themselves with the telephone.

"Hold on a minute." Excellent manners but not if the minute becomes ten or more with your correspondent waiting hopefully at several pence a minute. The least a trained telephonist should do is to "cut in" every minute explaining "sorry for the delay. Mr. Smith is now going to his room" or whatever. If a proper answer cannot be given to the caller it is not polite or decent to say, "Mr. Smith is out of the room, ring back in ten minutes". More correct in most circumstances is, "I will ask Mr. Smith to call you on his return; may I have your number?"

A word on how to answer a call initially may be valuable. What does the caller need to know first? In what order? Many people repeat their own number so the caller is aware of being "through" to the right place but why waste time? I prefer to give the name of my firm or organisation and perhaps say my own name, then "can I help you?" At home I may adopt a snappy approach such as "Jones' Home, Jean here" which puts any caller in the picture, or I give my name and "hello!" Avoid gruffness in your tone, even if it is an awkward moment.

Please don't waffle on and on if your listener is paying for the call. People notice.

For social calls especially, but sometimes in business, if you expect to have to talk for a long time, courtesy demands you enquire if it is convenient. Your listener might be starting a hot dinner or have a train to catch.

AVOID LIES, EVEN WHITE ONES

Top bracket people never ask their staff to say they are out, when they are in, and they don't lie themselves. Even so called white lies are often found out which is damaging to your reputation. Liars rarely get away with it in the long run.

18
SEX AND LOVE ETIQUETTE

Havelock Ellis said if all the energy, thought and activity surrounding love and sex were devoted to improving the world, it might be a wonderful place.

Shortly after being introduced to Anne Boleyn, with this excuse, if a king needs one, Shakespeare's Henry VIII said "It would be unmannerly were I to take you out and not to kiss you". The rascal king would have known that seeming courtesy can aid love. One selfish reason for politeness is that it could help a suitor, just as ill manners might hinder love. However, not all suitors are male, indeed there is a saying about a man marrying the girl who chooses him!

There is an unwritten law of love handed down the generations that it should be the man who initiates the early moves. This tradition is good for it fits in with nature: man usually being the more aggressive, woman more submissive. That there exist exceptions to this proves nothing. The exceptions are probably rarer than is thought, certainly fewer than is believed by some women's libbers.

The term sex equality is false for in the western world, there is really little or none. A woman is, on average, about 15% lighter in weight, needs less food and her brain is 15% smaller but that does not make it inferior. No man is 100% male nor is any woman all female. It follows that the majority of men are not fully aggressive, dashing or decisive and equally not every woman is totally submissive. It is possible that in the field of love things would have been easier if they had been, but we have to deal with what exists. However much some women may resent these views there is much truth in a saying which is worth giving thought to:

"Love is of man's life a thing apart,
'Tis woman's whole existence."

So – "vive la difference". It is part of woman's nature that she is less aggressive and the physical side of sex tends to remind her of her femininity. For the male penetrates whilst the female accepts is the way nature has arranged us. Without question the maternal instinct is strong in most women, though not in all. For women to feel inferior is wrong as one sex usually surpasses the other in different fields. Women, for example, may make superior doctors and everyone knows how wonderful they are as nurses and mothers. By nature, a woman is less endowed with muscle than a man but often she compensates with greater instinctive kindness and gentleness not to mention intuition. Men should never take advantage of their strength but it exists and has influence.

WHO LEADS IN MATTERS OF LOVE?

Customarily, early moves are made by the man and perhaps this has come about for the protection of women. In matters of love theories abound which cannot apply in every circumstance. One example is that men fall in love quickly and women slowly. But in life women often fall in love on sight just as most men tend to; equally many people do not know they are in love until after it has happened. Were it universally true that women fall slowly in love, this would be good. It would prevent them getting hurt so easily. This brings us nearer the etiquette of the matter for there is some wisdom in the view which I share that if she can prevent it a woman should not let herself fall too much in love with a man before he has declared his position. Another questionable theory (it actually shows more cynicism than sense) is that women suffer broken hearts more than men.

A man often kisses a girl good night after they go out the first time today, whereas years ago he probably did no more than peck her on the cheek, if that, until he had known her for weeks. The point about these kisses nowadays is that a girl should not imagine there is more in it than a kiss. Everyone has a fantasy side and it is at this point for either sex to practise mental discipline. In the early days of young people going out there is wisdom in their not taking it too seriously.

Men are often suspicious or afraid if they think a girl is "chasing" or "after" them because they believe it is their "right" to use the initiative. Psychologically they also probably need to be able to exert this maleness within the overall give and take of developing love. One could argue this puts the girl in a weaker position and while this may be true, as every mature girl knows there are many things she can do subtly, for example just happening to be near the man she favours rather frequently at work or play or wherever.

There is nothing impolite in a girl showing that she finds a man's company pleasing but she should show discretion.

"All is fair in love and war" is a widely believed saying. The emotion is so strong that people in love tend to be ruthless and selfish. Here manners play a part. The man and girl should consider the cost of causing unnecessary pain.

If a man wants to try and win a girl he must not be easily put off. He must persist without pestering, always within reason, and using art if he wishes to stay in the running. Men who have wooed girls for months, even years, have married and lived in bliss. The same applies the other way round. There have been many potential husbands who at first did not think an affair should continue who have in the end changed their minds.

Summing up, the man should, in the main, lead especially in the early days, but the woman may by her art manage to encourage him to think he is leading, even though it may not be strictly so. One reality seems to me to be that *some* leadership is vital, for love affairs which last *too long* without marriage, frequently end sadly: the weaker party usually being the sufferer.

It is often a problem of finding out why an affair is not maturing. An example could be a jealous third party turning one of the pair against the other. Another, that the man may prefer a thinner girl. Lots of girls have been able to do something about that and it may mean watching diet for life!

NEED FOR BRAKES

The word love is frequently abused when a young man says to a girl "I love you" almost from the first meeting. It may well be that he does not mean it. The use of the word "love" should be prudently reserved for later if it is found the friendship has meaning. If one partner employs the word too soon, the other should dismiss it from mind as probably being only a modern usage. If this is not done, much hurt could result. There is a great difference between loving someone and deciding if both have enough in common for marriage or a more permanent relationship. Given time, love affairs generally reach the conclusion that is best.

In love consideration for the other party is important. It is bad manners and morally evil for a man or woman to let the other think they are seriously in love if in their hearts they know all they want is friendship or only sex. Most people take their love affairs seriously and the agony of finding out that love is unrequited can cause untold unhappiness.

NEED FOR CAUTION BEFORE ENGAGEMENT

It is not always appreciated the extent that in matters of love emotion tends to overcome reason. The shock of being in love although not felt as shock, can sometimes mask this. Here, instinct is frequently – but not always – the best guide. A person can fall in love blindly and only much later do they suddenly see the whole picture, perhaps through dreams or in conscious thought. It is because of the strength of love that caution is necessary in the early stages. Neither side, but perhaps particularly the woman, should allow themselves to expect too much until they are sure of the other's true feelings.

It is good for an engagement to last for a few months which provides a cooling off period after the first passion of romance and allows the couple to regain their "sanity". Each will then discover if there is enough harmony of interest and background – so necessary as well as bodily attraction. People tend to rush through life, but in love matters, there is no wisdom in doing so only to repent during divorce proceedings.

Engagements That Go Wrong

A long engagement may be as risky as a short one but how does one end an engagement with the least pain? It could easily happen to an engaged couple that, later, without saying anything each of them realise they have chosen wrongly. The way to break an engagement is to do it as nicely and with as little hurt as possible. Perhaps a good way when one partner has decided going ahead would be foolish, is to write a brief letter expressing deep sorrow for wishing to break off the engagement and giving the main reasons Quite likely, the person at the receiving end has already realised that you were not suited.

The recipient of such a letter would I hope naturally want to be courteous and acknowledge it with regrets. Later the ring and any expensive gifts should be returned. That is one way but many could consider it is cowardly. I never believe in using courage unless one has to, but some people might prefer to visit their partner and explain while others may find it less distressing to break the news by telephone.

Another way a couple may part company is by not being available for a date here or there, perhaps being called away or even having to stay "late at work". Such methods may seem a bit thin but to be fair they can delay the break, so hopefully reducing its impact. Time usually proves a broken engagement was right.

Approaching the Altar

A lot is made about sex equality in friendships and marriage and girls rarely now use the old word obey in the marriage ceremony. Yet in all life most of us observe there have to be leaders and led for the best results. Leadership does not mean wife beating or bullying, simply that some times require one party, traditionally the man, to command. A wise man naturally leaves to his companion those fields where she is expert just as she would not interfere in areas which should belong to him. Many might *think* these ideas sexist or dated, but reality is different and behind the closed doors of the world one or other partner is usually head of the family. These remarks may apply to all types of couples, but obviously in good marriages there are almost never serious problems. Happiness is nearly all give and take, so beware an unbending attitude which makes a dangerous mate.

Good Manners In Courtship

If a man believes that he has found the right girl there may be problems still to come. His friend may well be afraid to show openly that she is enjoying his company and perhaps applicable to both sexes is a quotation from Ovid:

> "To sail swift ships,
> In chariots to ride,
> Require an Art
> No less is art love's guide."

The man has difficulty because by tradition he must inaugurate the affair but has to try to do it without over-declaring his feelings in case of hurting the girl's should he have to change his mind. Many men try to go too quickly before the girl has a chance to assess their qualities. My observation is that too much courage and speed have lost many males the girl of their choice. But undue hesitation can also lose. The saying about true love not running smoothly is an exaggeration. It is in our human frailty perhaps that the problem arises. The man has to act, rather than be himself: his sex drives him to make love at once perhaps even urges him towards seduction. Civilisation says "No, never, you must await the lady's pleasure." Television and films have taught millions about love and sex, and undoubtedly this has helped to reduce sex shyness, but has not solved every problem for many decent people. To hop into bed on the box appears easy and fun, but in life the opposite may be true. Television often provides a false picture.

GRAVE RISKS IN EXPERIMENTAL SEX

The advocates of experimental sex or free love probably rarely have to deal with the results of their advocacy. We may ignore warnings of the risks – which exist – of venereal disease, of becoming pregnant, of abortion or of unwanted births. The impression almost cultivated in much entertainment and modern writing is that there is no risk.

This false portrayal hides much danger. Not only television, but most of the media and sadly some doctors rarely mention venereal disease. This attitude is so widespread that the two most common infections, syphilis and gonorrhoea are often now referred to along with other illnesses or diseases as S.T.D. This stands for "sexually transmitted diseases". The term may help reduce feelings of guilt which society inflicts upon those contracting venereal diseases, but the diseases may rampage all the more while the public are "protected" from awareness of their serious nature.

Syphilis and gonorrhoea *are the commonest venereal diseases and are both fully curable if treated adequately and early enough.* The same, unfortunately, cannot be said, of A.I.D.S. (Acquired Immune Deficiency Syndrome), which came to light in the early 1980s and has been increasing at an exponential rate all over the world. Since this virus is of recent advent, it has not been possible to study the epidemic over long periods, and new discoveries are being made about it all the time. What is known so far is that (a) in those who develop the full syndrome it is incurable and invariably fatal eventually, (b) many people are infected and may never develop the full syndrome, but they can still infect others, who may develop AIDS with fatal results, (c) it is a blood disease which works by attacking the body's immune system, (d) it is spread venereally but also by direct infection (e.g. drug addicts sharing needles), (e) in the early stages of the epidemic in Europe and North America it has spread mainly among the homosexual communities, but in Africa the spread seems to be equal in both sexes.

To put it bluntly, since the mid-1980s, the practice of "sleeping around" carries with it the serious possibility of a premature but lingering death. This fact demands a major change from the moral values of the "swinging" '60s and '70s.

The contraceptive pill, although almost 100% effective in preventing conception *when used correctly*, has created problems. *One of the most serious is that it gives no protection against venereal infections.* There are a number of other risks as the pill does not physically suit some people but perhaps the chief one is that the instructions given are not always carried out. This may explain why there are still a large number of illegitimate births and abortions.

An important difference between the pill or other methods used by the female and the sheath, is that the latter, although not 100% safe as birth control, is an important factor in the prevention of sexually transmitted diseases. This is mentioned because many girls who are living with men are worried and fearful – not without reason (or vice versa of course). Unfortunately, men are not saints nor are women nuns, and there are partners who are promiscuous without admitting it, hence the need to mention the male preventative. The sheath, if undamaged and carefully used is a considerable protection against disease. In marriage the incidence of promiscuity is less because of guilt feelings and circumstances, which apply less to a pre-marital affair, particularly one which may be temporary.

Historically, contraception was used to prevent having too many children, or for some reason for not wanting to have any. Birth control helped to ameliorate the social problems of illegitimacy. That in brief was the position up to about the late 1950s. Married people legitimately requiring them could obtain contraceptives while for others and for children, it was almost impossible.

We should understand the change which then took place. The almost unfettered availability of contraception wasn't the only phenomenon. A gigantic sex *industry*, like the race relations industry, grew up and there were school lectures, school writers on sex, booklets issued, even encouragement given to children before they were ready to receive it. Pornographic sex aid shops invaded our towns, all aimed to stimulate in this matter, which has vast ramifications as well as dangers.

Mrs. Whitehouse has talked more wisdom than a lot of the sly or permissive types who, underneath their veneer, know the subject is one in which they can earn a jolly good living or much publicity without hard work. Such types thus follow in the footsteps of the world's oldest profession, so helping to spread disease (and pregnancy) for no entirely safe contraception exists. On the whole, all this causes long-term misery, none the less miserable, because it is often hidden from view. Books on sex are still in print which scarcely even mention V.D.; the impression being given that it does not exist. Many T.V. programmes indicate that sex in bed is one long *risk-free pleasure.*

Top Harley Street doctors (still probably the world's best) will tell you of some of the results of the new permissiveness. The increase in the incidence of syphilis and gonorrhoea is one, and the new scourge of AIDS another. The increase in herpes – an illness which though not dangerous to life can be most intractable – can be directly attributed to multiple sexual liaisons. Recent evidence is tending to confirm that cervical cancer is caused by a virus and that there is a statistical relationship between youthful promiscuity and later development of this illness. Some doctors are describing this as a "cancer explosion".

What has all this to do with etiquette? Several things. Firstly the pill now being available to over 16s and even under-age children in some instances, tends to encourage casual sex indulgence. Yet while it is expected that adolescents should change boy or girl friends frequently – after all it is their nature to find their way in love, as in all things – they have not always been cautioned about uninhibited sex. That a sexual appetite shouldn't be allowed to eclipse true caring for another person, as it so easily can, is conveniently ignored.

A generation or two back, the unmarried – at least in the middle classes – usually stopped short of intercourse, reserving this for the marriage bed. Instead, people made do with what was called in the 'thirties "heavy petting".

Earlier generations *did consider* each other's welfare in pre-pill days, giving consideration pride of place, above possibly short term satisfactions. The same attitude is needed again today, now that the prospect of fatal infection has reared its head.

Debate about permissiveness being all right if the pair love each other has always been a white washing excuse for fornication. The argument not only ignores the risks of infections, it does not hold either when you allow that "affairs" break up more often than marriages. Extra marital lovers too are not always sincere (the promiscuous ones) and there are increasing thousands of people carrying and passing on AIDS who do not know it, or couldn't care less anyway. So the diseases and tragedy which often result can honestly be described as the *worst of bad manners*. Remember the definition "thoughtfulness for others..."

Permissiveness has resulted in a loss of discipline not only in sex but in all areas, yet, without discipline civilised life would become impossible. Its predictable outcome – making divorce easy as well – has not universally brought greater happiness either, although that was the intention.

Recently, to be fair, excessive permissiveness has come under attack. It is interesting that the country which first encouraged sexual freedom in the West, Sweden, is now changing course. The Swedes who first advocated free love and pornography have now, in the 1980s, realised the enormous damage their theories have created. Those who were pioneering free love there have now turned completely and are attacking the thing which they introduced and supported.

HOW FAR TO GO – LIVING TOGETHER

In any sex relationship, as we have implied, etiquette demands that the man and the girl should be frank. As love develops, the pair should reach firm decisions regarding the extent to which they intend to go. Considerate people should talk frankly about their position and explain whether they are interested in each other mainly for friendship (platonic), or with a hope of marriage. The coming of the pill, and the subsequent increased danger of venereal disease, have both caused a change in outlook. The problem of people for whom the pill is merely an excuse for irresponsible and casual sex, is a real one.

There are instances where marriage may be impossible (or impossible for the time being) and many people today argue that those in such positions should live together. Nowadays, sharing of life openly by unmarried people is widespread. Such lifestyles may seem distasteful but to "judge" *can be just as inappropriate*. Here therefore we touch on moral (and medical) aspects only in so far as they affect our subject.

People genuinely hoping to marry soon, often wonder if they should anticipate marriage fully and many do. Because of the (supposed safety of the) pill, the tendency has been to sleep together more than would have happened in pre-pill days. Then, there was a definite line between what formerly was called flirting or wooing and anticipating marriage. It is worth taking into account, before agreeing on whether to indulge fully before marriage, that it can make an engagement more fragile than it might be. The fear of mishap is not a good basis for long term love.

Nevertheless for all the pros and cons a decision still has to be reached by each couple, whether they will sleep together before marrying, using the sheath, or whether they will stop short of intercourse. Crudely, the choice may lie between pre-marital intercourse and what earlier generations called "heavy petting" which was widely indulged in.

The pressures towards giving way to intercourse are greater now but if a couple choose to, they can find satisfaction, without full intercourse and thus some of the risks are eliminated. Although there is arguably now a healthier outlook on sex than in post-

Victorian times, considerate people should ponder whether things have gone too far not only because of the physical risks but because of the effect on the personalities of the participants.

In addition, perhaps *above all*, if we decide to risk creation of a new life, should come our consideration of our responsibility for that life. Before the step is taken, do we both agree to a commitment to bring up the child and thus to marriage? Or do we choose to accept that abortion with its dangers and ethics might be an allowable alternative? These are among the questions it would be presumptuous for any book to answer – for each the answer must be their own.

THE GIRL'S PART

On getting to know each other here are a few extra words. A woman should never play "hard to get", by, for example, being booked (unless it is true). This technique is based on a fallacy. It may work well in the bedroom as part of precoital love-play within marriage, so important to sexual arousal and happiness, but that does not mean it wins in courting. It is a false method easily seen through and leaving the question – "why deceive?" – in the man's mind.

Another aspect of the male's traditional role as initiator is important because, in general, if a girl does not accept being kissed or having her hand held by the man, it may allow her to signal he is not the one for her. Whilst a man has the privilege to initiate the cuddling, the girl has the right, which must be regarded as sacred, to say "Stop, no further". Her lover must obey. Complicating such moments girls sometimes pretend they don't want something when in their hearts they do and the man has to judge the situation. Similarly if the girl is encouraging him, which as the affair develops she is entitled to, he has to assess whether she is serious or not.

KISS AND DON'T TELL

Never tell outsiders any details of your affair. This is the worst of manners and a phrase might be coined:

"Never kiss and tell
For that is the road to hell."

PLATONIC FRIENDSHIPS

Platonic male and female friendships are common despite some maintaining this to be impossible. Many men and girls have a companionship without a whiff of sex purely for convenience and sharing happiness. They may come to an arrangement to go to parties together, join groups and the like, even perhaps sharing a flat or agreeing to help each other find a suitable marriage partner or permanent boy or girl friend. Why not?

DIFFERENT LOVE

Homosexuality and lesbianism are less common in reality than in films or books. Far more common are men or women who indulge as a substitute or for fun. All of us are to some extent bi-sexual, but it is foolish for anyone to encourage any tendency in this direction lightly. For one thing it might become a habit and even today there is a risk of blackmail. True homosexuality is rare but not necessarily a sign of weakness or illness if the individual adjusts mentally.

It is not, perhaps, generally known that venereal disease has for some time been far more common among male homosexuals. But everybody knows that AIDS first became common in the "gay" community. Both these facts are probably due to the *very* large number of different partners that some homosexuals have – this has enabled AIDS to spread with frightening rapidity. Government health warnings should be heeded.

19
DOCTOR-PATIENT RELATIONSHIP

The doctor-patient relationship is more one of ethics than of etiquette. *Medical etiquette* is concerned rather with the code of behaviour *between* medical people which doctors learn in their training. The ethics come into the matter in regard to behaviour between patients and other people, where a doctor is often called upon to offer guidance or help. As this is of great importance, readers should also refer to the previous chapter where medical problems of contraception and sex are dealt with. Also see chapter 24.

MALE OR FEMALE DOCTOR
A doctor visiting or being visited by a patient of the opposite sex ought to have someone (nurse or receptionist for example) around. This is specially so for men doctors examining female patients, otherwise they run the risk of being accused or blackmailed. This does happen rather more than news reports of it are seen.

THE RULE OF CONFIDENTIALITY
Doctors are in receipt of a lot of information of a confidential nature and their work utterly depends on trust. A modern headache for our doctors is the (under the age of consent) girl of maybe 12, or 15, who having read or heard discourses on sex churned out by the latest pseudo-scientific glossies, or broadcast debates, or school instructors, demands the latest pill or vaginal foam, so she can run with the "Jones" boys and girls. The unfortunate family doctor is put in a difficult position if the girl has not told her parents. His examination of the child could result in his being accused of indecent assault. Prescribing the pill to a girl under 16 is dangerous because of the possible serious effects to the immature body and mind.

No girl, with possible rare exceptions, should be so inconsiderate as to ask her doctor to provide birth control, unless her parents approve and give their approval in writing. The doctor should persuade the child to tell her parents. Even agreement of course does not alter the risk of the child becoming promiscuous, as children are more apt to be. That's the problem for doctor, parent and child. The ethics in this matter are not clearly defined nor is the legal position, so the doctor faces an unfair dilemma if the child insists. He could refuse to prescribe but that makes problems too.

One ethical problem which doctors face is where a man or girl has V.D., perhaps contracted after only one "wild night", and the sufferer will not tell his spouse because of fear for their relationship. The doctor should do his utmost to get the innocent party in for tests and endeavour to prevent the infected party from intercourse till cured; otherwise the danger of great tragedies arises. Confidence and truth are a doctor's most powerful weapons.

Digressing slightly, as the matter is often not mentioned; briefly, the symptoms to watch for are, for syphillis any spots or pimples usually on or around the sex parts, while for gonorrhoea any feeling of "burning" in the urethra, especially on passing water and maybe a slight discharge, inflammation or irritation. These symptoms for the former may not appear for some weeks whilst for gonorrhoea they may show in days. Detection is not always easy and for the woman often very difficult – hence our suggestion of a check-up with your doctor or at a special V.D. clinic if one has been exposed to risk. They are contact diseases almost never contracted outside intercourse. Another reason for a check-up is that sometimes the symptoms are so slight as not to be noticed.

Confidence Absolute

A good doctor hears many things, for patients confess their sins to him and many a marriage, for example, would have broken up if the doctor had leaked his secrets. These he must hold in trust. Neither must he tell nor ever be expected to do so.

Next of kin or whoever is in charge of a patient, must be given the necessary facts to treat an illness but no one should expect a doctor to discuss his patients' complaints or diseases.

SOCIAL FRIENDSHIPS

Patients often place their doctor on a pedestal and perhaps rightly. Our doctors, speaking generally and our bookmakers (this may shock a few people) are probably among the last remaining groups in twentieth century society who retain the integrity (whatever other faults they may have) for which Britain was once renowned.

While it is sometimes done to invite your doctor to join your parties or visit you socially, it is usually unwise. It can spoil the relationship and just as it is often better not to do business with friends, similarly it is generally wiser to keep your medical life and friendships separate. It frequently happens that a doctor has some sad or difficult things to tell his patients and this can be easier in a more formal relationship. So if your doctor refuses that invitation don't think he is merely being ill mannered!

20
THE DRUG AND DRINK PROBLEM

The strain of living must perhaps be connected with soaring alcoholism, as a means of escape from reality or sometimes sadness though it may not be the only cause. Unfortunately, Home Office figures show an even larger percentage growth in the abuse of drugs. The scene has changed from years ago when police found drug taking largely confined to the young in public places, like discos. Recent raids on houses have discovered drug abuse and cannabis cultivation becoming more common and the ages of those trafficking or becoming addicted, older. It has been said "there are *no old* addicts!"

Many people have grown up without ever being offered a drug or known any takers. Lucky people. The writer has known several young people between 16 and 32 who come of good, Christian, middle or upper class families who are now addicts with little hope of cure.

What can happen is that at parties, someone gets hold of some drug or other, and for a lark, or experiment passes the drug round or even worse secretly puts it into a friend's drink or food. A man down from University told me recently that even among the educationally privileged who were there, drug abuse was a serious problem in certain groups. Such an extreme view is based on personal experience which would not apply to well balanced young people. Yet the existence of such a view is alarming. The drug "industry" is enormous and one can see the degradation of it in some areas of our cities. Young addicts in our streets were a sight unknown a few decades ago.

No one with a pretence of being well-bred, or a Christian will ever take part in what could be called the fourth addiction (drink, promiscuity and smoking being the other three. Did someone say gluttony?) It is a crime to do so and while the thought of telling on others is abhorrent to a Britisher, so appalling are the end results that decent citizenship demands that any information known or discovered about drug selling should be passed, confidentially or anonymously, to the police.

THE DRINKER

I suspect there are two main types of people in danger from drinking. The more common is the one who continuously increases his intake so that he finds himself *hurrying* home at night for that pre-meal gin or whisky. Such people hate to be told they are alcoholics but they are and many such can still stop by will power. It is the excess drinking which kills and it kills just as often whether named social drinking or not.

The second type, is the person who by his nature is *sensitive* to drink to *such an extent* that even after a few drinks he may be hooked. Anyone who feels in this category should apply immediate will power and stick to tomato juice or soft drinks. To win such a battle against such an addiction is a challenge worth taking up.

21
LETTERS OF SYMPATHY FOR A DEATH, FUNERAL CUSTOMS AND OTHER LETTERS

Writing a letter of sympathy needs skill if it is to be effective. One risk in sending several pages in an attempt to convey sympathy is that it could be misunderstood. Possibly it is best to begin by giving a few lines of sympathy and for most people the shorter this part of the letter the less likely it is to be misinterpreted.

There are times when sympathy can be expressed verbally or by telephone but this may be difficult and many people are so heartbroken that it is unwise to use any method other than a letter. Following a death some funeral announcements expressly request "no letters" and this must be honoured. But your best friends may need *more* than a letter. You may be the right person to help them grieve and they can't spill out sorrow onto a letter. Sometimes a condolence call is the only appropriate tribute. What, after all, is friendship if it is not "in deed" at such a time?

Death is usually a heart-rending time and a strain for everybody. This means that relatives and friends should show consideration and sympathy for those who are bereaved. It is generally unwise to try to help the next-of-kin or whoever is in charge unless you are asked, but if you feel help might be required then an offer is appropriate. Care is needed to avoid seeming to interfere which could cause distress. On hearing of a death you may consider making a phone call (post being too slow) of sympathy, offering help, for example, with transport to the funeral or accommodation for any mourners for a night. If living nearby it could be nicer to drop a note in rather than disturb the distressed.

LETTERS OF SYMPATHY
The use of "My dear" indicates sympathy and should be used if you know the recipient well. If the letter goes to several people, the

next-of-kin's name, e.g. the wife's name, would come first, then the eldest son, etc.

Here is a letter to relatives of *someone old* who has died.

> Dear X,
>
> We are all sad to hear of the sudden death of your mother. What can we say, except that we all loved her, and express our deepest sympathy. Our youngsters often spoke to her on the way to school and she will be greatly missed in the neighbourhood. She was so understanding, generous and cheerful.
>
> May God be with you and yours at this time of mourning and if there is anything we can do to assist, please ask.
>
> With our deep sympathy at this heartbreaking time.
>
> Yours sincerely,
>
> Y and Z

The above letter could be longer. One has to decide on the situation which exists. Usually with neighbours or acquaintances a short letter expressing deepest sympathy is probably enough with, in suitable circumstances, an offer to help.

As these letters are difficult for most of us, here is a specimen to the family on the death of the father.

> My dear A and B,
>
> All of us here have loved knowing your wonderful father. We pray that in God's good time all distress will diminish and pass as I am sure your father would have wished. We have had so many enjoyable times in your home that it is a very sad day for us too.
>
> With our deepest sympathy and love to you all,
>
> Yours very sincerely,

Letters may not be required in all instances. If you all meet regularly, for example in an office or a club, perhaps a hand-shake and a few words of sympathy such as "I was very sorry to learn of your father/mother/sister's death. We will certainly miss him/her" may be sufficient depending on your relationship with those concerned. Again, sympathy may be expressed by telephone. If one has been at the funeral then neither letters nor telephone messages are so essential but it is usually nicer to write as well.

Here is a letter on the death of a friend.

My dear A,

I was distressed to hear the sad news. May I say these few things. Paul was my friend, and he always stood by me in good weather or bad. Paul did not know what it was to run away from any problem.

He had a great big brave and willing heart and he died without knowing how ill he was which I am sure was the way he would have loved to go. However, I know he did not want to pass on leaving Jean on her own. He loved life too much to have thought of leaving it yet but at least he has been spared prolonged suffering.

If you feel there is any way I can help you, do ask and may God be with you in these days of sadness but I know Paul would not expect any sadness. He wanted everyone to be happy and to live fully.

> With our love,
> Yours very sincerely,

Another sample letter on the death of a young wife where the grandparents of the children live in the house too.

My dearest Ralph and family,

William's heart and mine bleed for all of you, but especially for you and the children.

We cannot understand why such sad things happen. It is not possible in any words to convey our sympathy but we can say this. We can ask God to give you what we all need at such times in great quantity – courage, which I know you have, full faith, hope and belief for the future.

I am sure your dear wife would have wished you all to recover quickly from the shock. Life is mysterious but one thing is immortal and wonderful and I refer to the inheritance cards in each of your youngsters. All have parts of you and of their mother which, although in diminishing quantities, will be passed on while life on earth lasts. To me, it is facts such as this which prove there is a God and which are more wonderful than landing on the moon.

There exists something else beyond science which so often happens and I believe in. It is that a special strength, both spiritual and bodily, seems to be given – God-given – to those who are in great need. Our prayer is that you all as well as your parents and your wife's parents will receive this in full measure from that power beyond, which none of us can fully understand.

    With our deepest sympathy and love,

                Yours very sincerely,

(or) your Uncle/cousin or X,

MEMORIAL SERVICE

I was recently at a Memorial Service and came across the following paragraph which seems to me so nice to be used in any way in connection with a death. Here it is:—

"Death is nothing at all . . . I have only slipped away into the next door room – I am I and you are you . . . Whatever we were to each other, that we are still. Call me by my old familiar name, speak to me in the easy way which you always used. Put no difference into your tone; wear no forced air of solemnity or sorrows. Laugh as we always laughed at the little jokes we enjoyed together. Play, smile, think of me, pray for me. Let my name be ever the household word that it always was. Let it be spoken without effect, without the ghost of a shadow on it. Life means all that it ever meant, it is the same as it ever was; there is absolutely unbroken continuity. What is this death, but a neglible accident? Why should I be out of mind, because I am out of sight? I am but waiting for you, for an interval. Somewhere very near just around the corner . . . All is well.

                – Henry Scott Holland (1847-1918)
                Canon of St. Paul's Cathedral"

AT AND AFTER A FUNERAL

The custom at funerals is usually that at the end of the service all present shake hands with the next of kin and possibly close relatives without speaking, or simply saying "I'm so sorry" or maybe "We loved Catherine/Gerald". In sad circumstances frequently the least said is wise. It is a time for tears not words.

Often, especially in Wales or Scotland but also in many other parts of Britain several of those attending the funeral or if there are not too many, all of them, may be asked round to the house afterwards for tea or perhaps even a high tea. Drinks may be served later and nowadays a death is regarded more as a passing on, people realising that life has to begin anew both on earth and hereafter. The deceased may even have expressed the wish that there is to be "no sadness". (See also Chapter 12)

EXPRESSING SYMPATHY, CONGRATULATIONS, ETC.

Other letters of condolence, congratulation or best wishes may be required. Examples would be a niece passing an exam, or a friend failing his second driving test.

Birthdays of young relations or dear friends call loudly for a good wishes note, or birthday card with a personal message added or at least a 'phone call. Everyone likes to be remembered. The younger ones adore an enclosure whether it be an edible gift or a toy, or for an older child, money. Recall your own young days how nice these things were. They are especially acceptable in this cruel world, so do maintain a list to remind you of important dates for birthdays, anniversaries, etc. Children rarely forget people who are kind and generous to them and it all helps to make life that little bit more fun. Adults too should not be forgotten.

Such letters are easy to write, in addition to the main point, unlike letters of sympathy, any interesting news can be added to fill the page or more.

If you are worried over *any* letter, two good tests are 1) leave it for a day or if possible a little longer because then you become fishy-eyed and will probably spot any poor style or errors.
2) read it out loud to yourself; if it sounds right it is probably excellent; an even better tip is to have someone read it to you whilst you listen to its "flow". Professional writers often use these tricks; ideally a gap between readings of at least one week is best but that would be impossible for letters of sympathy.

LETTERS TO THE SICK

Accidents happen. People take ill and letters of sympathy are required but these need not be sad and the main purpose of such messages is to cheer someone who is having a bad time. Letters to an invalid, apart from expressing the hope that they are not in pain and will get well soon, can include newsy items, perhaps jokes, photographs or humorous stories. They are good for somebody who is a long distance away as it is not always possible to telephone people in hospital, but even if they are nearby they can be useful because visiting times may be restricted.

Letters help to brighten the day. There is no doubt that, especially the old who may have few friends still alive are made happier by receiving longish letters and perhaps interesting cuttings from the press whether from relatives or others.

Many situations requiring sympathy can be dealt with by telephone, for instance one may have to express sympathy or regrets by saying to a friend "Sorry you did not pass your exam but it is not a matter of life and death and I hope you will be lucky next time". None of us like to be forgotten when fate has been unkind.

Sample letter to an old friend who is emigrating:

My dear Bill,

I have just heard from your cousin that you are about to leave for New Zealand. You have been one of my greatest friends and I shall miss you.

You do know that you will always be most welcome to stay with us when you return on holiday.

Meanwhile, best of luck and Godspeed, and we shall look forward to hearing of your progress.

With our greetings,

Sincerely yours,

The following letter could be written to an employee on leaving:

My dear Mrs. Brown,

I am writing on behalf of all of us here to say goodbye and to wish you great happiness in your retirement.

It is always sad to part after so many years with so good and faithful an ambassador for our company.

Well done, and while memory lasts we will think, from time to time, of the great Mrs. Brown. The enclosed cheque is but a token and everyone joins in saying "Good fortune and may long life and happiness be yours".

Yours very sincerely,

J. R. Black,
For all at X.

THANKS

Times change and probably most thanks are given by telephone but a newish custom has developed since telephoning costs mounted and it saves time if there is no reply to the 'phone call. Neighbours just pop a thank you card or notelet through the door. From further afield you would use the post.

Here are some thank yous for different situations:

Dear Jean and Bill,

Where did you learn to entertain? From the moment we reached your home we realised that it was going to be one of those lovely parties which so rarely happen. You do have charming friends and my sister and I loved every minute. We thought the card game helped to get things going. You must have been busy producing the lovely food and "the" party will long stay in our happy memory.

> Again, thanks and greetings,
>
> Sincerely yours,

Letters may be shorter and another sample might be:

My dear X,

Just a line to say how kind it was of you to have our two children stay the night while we were away. I hope they behaved and I need hardly tell you that if you ever wish us to do the same for you it will be a pleasure. The kids loved being with you. Our greetings and thanks.

> Yours sincerely,
>
> John and Jill.

Sadly not everyone bothers with thank yous these days but perhaps the reason for this change is that there is less humbug, and a number of people take the view "well, we thanked our friends profusely when we left, it is silly to bother them with letters". However, one polite way of taking the lazier route is to say as you leave when expressing thanks (which of course is essential) "We won't write as we have thanked you now" and leave it at that. For any costly or big entertainment a letter should be sent.

After a group holiday a note to the organiser is never out of place. Adopt a friendly, punchy and flattering style if you like, to lift it out of the ordinary run-of-the-mill thank you:

Dear Robert,

Correction "BERTIE",

Alexander Graham Bell went to America to feel free to develop the telephone; Charles Darwin selected the BEAGLE to work out his evolution revolt; Robert J. Henderson harnessed to Corfu, *the* holiday.

Do not imagine these words exaggerate. Only such can present my heartfelt thanks in a fitting tribute to your efforts which blended such magic days for us all. Next year beckons.

> Appreciatively,
>
> Charlie.

To a house-help who is retiring:

Dear Mary,

You have worked for us longer than anyone and John and I look on you more as a friend than an employee. While memory lasts, neither of us will forget all the laughter, fun and talks we had with you. We will miss you.

May you live long to enjoy all the years ahead with your wonderful family, sisters and friends. We shall think of you often. The children also send you their greetings and good wishes. From our hearts we say good luck and do keep in touch. This invites you to join us every year for Christmas drinks.

The enclosed gift is only a token of our esteem and love.

Yours very sincerely,

OTHER LETTERS

Dear . . . . . .

Thank you both for a very enjoyable evening — nice having a foursome — more chance to catch up on family news.

I love your new home, so compact, yet has everything. Super meal — I enjoyed every bit of it and I know Bill did, even to being "piggy" over your chocolates.

Our love and greetings.

Affectionately yours,

Dear . . . . . .

The children and staff of XYZ School would like to thank you from the bottom of our hearts for your kind donation of books to use in our Grand Fete on May 27th.

We had a very enjoyable day and made £650 for the school fund. Once again thank you very much.

Yours faithfully,

Headmistress.

22
JUDGING PEOPLE BY ETIQUETTE

Confidence tricksters and crooks usually show almost impeccable etiquette. This is interesting because successful criminals are often so intelligent they could make excellent livings in many trades, yet they choose crime. They sense that if they are polite, appear well-bred and well-dressed they are likely to bring off that profitable but dishonest deal. So beware of excessive etiquette.

Conversely by watching a person's manners, with the above exceptions, one can tell a lot about them. Good breeding is not a term I like yet there is something in a person's bearing and the way they dress which, 99 times out of 100, indicates much about them.

If you show a lady into a lounge and she sits with her back to the light, alone that would not indicate good manners but if the same woman sat at your table and held her knife and fork correctly, then you could be fairly sure she had come of a good family. The reason for a woman sitting with her back to the light is that any facial blemishes or wrinkles show up less, similarly some no longer young women prefer candlelight for a dinner party. Vanity has its harmless place. Cater for it.

Also if she ate her soup correctly (for some reason unknown to me it is correct to sup soup using the spoon away from your body, whereas if you are eating a sweet you bring the spoon towards you), this would be an additional pointer to the person's background.

As a top person however you don't carry etiquette on your sleeve. Most people recognise by instinct a lady or gentleman on sight and it has more to do with their poise, the way the person walks and behaves, than the cost of their car. Our manners and thoughtfulness towards them tell others a great deal about us.

COURTESIES WHICH INDICATE GOOD MANNERS
Women's lib or no, people with good manners are invariably courteous. Thus, for example, if two or three men were sitting in a lounge and a married couple entered, or for that matter a single

person of either sex, it is customary for those already there to stand up as a form of greeting and welcome. It helps greatly if the host says something like "come along and join us" or "welcome John, have a seat" and introduces as required. This enables the group to relax and continue conversation. Sometimes the person entering may acknowledge the gesture with a quick "don't get up!" to forestall people's kindness, thus returning the courtesy.

Another point worth mentioning is that if a woman rises to leave the room it is old-world courtesy for a man to open the door if he is near and this would also apply to elderly people of either sex. At one time if there were perhaps four of five men in a room and a woman acquaintance entered or wanted to leave it, everyone tended to leap up like jumping jacks. This excessive reaction has been largely dropped. As habits and customs change so have the more rigid forms of etiquette been abandoned as people become easier in their relationships. However, lapses in these minor courtesies have, I feel, been too great in recent years. At least a partial return of their elegant niche in society would be welcome but the fussy manners of more formal times are out of place today especially among old friends.

CONVERSATIONS

Emerson remarked that with good friends there is no need for second thought while discoursing with them. If you have known someone a long time and are on good terms people can and do say almost anything they think, even if it may be a little shocking, even personal. But one needs to temper one's remarks to suit particular people. I have dear friends with whom I chatter almost without thinking or fear of offending but I also have old friends of both sexes with whom I have to exercise tact. Some people are sensitive and not all of us have philosophic corners into which to retreat if someone says something the meaning of which may be slightly insulting. My reaction to anyone who told me I was a fool is simply that I have always known this. With healthy-minded people some leg-pulling and fun poking adds spice. "A little nonsense now and then is relished by the wisest men" so long as care is exercised not to offend. If a person does take a wrong meaning out of a remark, a profuse apology generally suffices.

The courtesies of life help to make it pleasant in many spheres but I confess I cannot understand why when a politician refers to another he calls him "The Honourable Gentleman". How many have much honour about them? Perhaps the reason for using such flattery is that it may prevent some of these chaps from spouting statistics, or "lies" and "damned lies" too often!

Avoiding politics and religion in conversation is an old rule of manners mentioned earlier but recently, perhaps because politics, and to some extent, religion, have got into everything, this rule is somewhat relaxed. Nonetheless, in top ten company, good talkers, certainly if these subjects bore, can guide the talk into more interesting fields. On these subjects people often become heated so politics or religion and too much weather, should be discouraged. At parties folk want to get away into an atmosphere of fun, good tales well told and of interest.

LEG PULLING

Fun is fun in this British pastime, but don't pull legs too hard for even those who appear to enjoy this have feelings. Jokes too that are too crude, while often indulged in with men, are avoided in mixed company or where there are children.

SPORTING COURTESIES

In sport it is a nice custom to make a point of thanking your opponents and also your partner or team-mates at the end of the game. Some of us may smile at footballers who, after scoring, hug and kiss, but it makes the world go round.

On the other hand, at the end of a day's shooting or fishing one would not go round and thank one's fellow sportsmen – other than the host – though appreciative guests invariably make a point of thanking the ghillie or the keeper and some or all the beaters for the enjoyable day.

BE DISCREET

Discretion is an important part of polite living. There are old sayings deserving respect among which are "Speak no ill of the dead" and "he who laughs last, laughs longest" etc.

A friend of the author happened to be visiting a club to which he belonged when he was button-holed by a girl whom he knew only slightly. Unfortunately she was drunk and also a nymphomaniac. Being kind he didn't like to cut her as she was a neighbour but she took advantage of the situation and began clinging to him and trying to kiss him. My friend thought no more of it. Months later my friend and his wife gave a party to which *another* woman who had seen the husband with the drunk woman in the club, was invited. On arrival, speaking loudly, in front of my friend's wife and guests, she said "And how is the sexy girl friend I saw you with in the X club?" This woman was never invited back but what she didn't know was that my friend had the last laugh. He had anticipated that there was a slim chance she might mention the matter so had warned his wife. No harm was done, but it could have caused trouble and was appalling manners.

BEWARE OF GOSSIPS

Occasions arise where a man may take a colleague's or neighbour's wife to a concert or something of mutual interest. When this is done the man should first obtain the husband's permission but even so, human nature being what it is, as well as the habit of gossip, it may be folly. Certainly if done often it can end in disaster. The freedom of the sexes operates better in theory than in practice.

DISGUSTING HABITS

If you must chew gum do it in privacy, and the same applies to picking your nose! Spit only at the dentist's and never in public places unless you are alone.

LAPSUS LINGUAE

These happen, funny or otherwise! Few of us get through life without making some slips of the tongue. An example was when a young man was dancing with a girl to whom he was attracted. This girl had a prettier sister who did not happen to attract my friend. In his excitement, as it was one of his first dances, he said to his partner, trying to break the ice, "some people think your sister Jean is prettier than you". The girl lost her temper and administered a severe kick on his shin! That was extreme; normally people don't react so violently and if a mistake is made they accept apologies and forget. This is good advice. Minor human errors are not the end of the world.

DON'T BE SHY

Shyness is self-curable if the shy person can change his/her philosophy of life and learn to laugh at any errors he/she may make in conversation. People can also develop the art of talking to strangers and helping others by so doing. (See also chapters 1 & 2.)

Once again "thoughtfulness for others is the essence . . ." and here in practice, shy people by developing their conversation, be it through small talk, or even chatting about simple things like holidays or offering to help a stranger or a foreigner, can do so much. Not only to help themselves and enrich their lives but to make things nicer for those around whether they be fellow countrymen or visitors.

One could argue it is not that simple to change from being shy to an extrovert but it can be done. Many an extrovert today is a former introvert who by his efforts has pulled himself out of the self-imposed loneliness of the shy.

THE MOODY NON-CO-OPERATIVE BRIGADE!

They say men do not die, they kill themselves. There exist millions of moody people; people who fail to co-operate with others and who are killing themselves spiritually. Unless they are in a good mood and feeling well, they sulk into themselves. To their recipients (of ill boding) it seems like a form of running away from normality and life. It may arise in (clinical) depression, for which there is at least some excuse (so long as efforts are in train to reach a cure) but otherwise one wonders if such folk realise that they may be demonstrating pitiful manners – which make life sad for those near or dear to them. It is because of the importance of this matter that it is given a heading of its own. This moodiness is found everywhere, on boats, at the bridge table, in the office, factory and home.

Unpleasant as sulky habits and grumpiness are for others what such people are probably doing for themselves is laying the foundations of their own misery *but it is important not to judge.* For example disabled folk may have every excuse for depressing sunken moods (though it is not usually to them we refer) or spare a thought for the possibility that the person is depressively disabled. With depression being an unseen illness it is especially galling for depressives to find themselves defenceless outcasts of society's normally enjoyable social mixing. Most such people can improve themselves by thinking hopefully and with medical advice but you can help them regain happiness too. Include them. Listen to them. Remember, "there but for the grace of God . . .".

Happiness Is Free

Millions seem to expect the world to owe them happiness but it only provides the opposite. I knew a girl who was flat chested, had lost an eye, which made her appear to squint, and had about everything against her in life. Well, she made a decision, viz that she would smile at her troubles, become a co-operator and help all with whom she had contacts. She dropped the reasons for being unhappy –

replacing the negatives with positives and by her kindness and charm made for herself a beautiful life, mothered several children and she and her husband found that happiness which is beyond price.

If you always feel moody, it may have a physical or mental cause, spare no effort to find a good doctor who should provide treatment, so that a new page can, hopefully, be turned over and a fresh life developed to replace the old.

Good V Bad Moods

We all have good moods and bad moods but the manners and disciplines which ought to have been taught us at home and school should mean that any bad tempers are short lived. Outrageous or insulting behaviour can hurt everyone within range but particularly the *instigator*. Thus, as the author of the classic, The Last Enemy, found out, the enemy was himself. It needed greatness to discover and then months to re-build happiness anew.

We often have much to put up with, or are perhaps treated unfairly or may be the victim of malicious gossip – possibly even true gossip for truth can hurt perhaps more.

Such things are best ignored; many a time the author has consoled herself by recalling that old Chinese proverb, "if a man spit upon you, let it dry". To return the spit is beyond the pale.

SPORTSMANSHIP AT ITS BEST

Many years ago Bobby Jones won most of the main golf championships and those who watched him play realised that he was courteous not only to the crowd but to his opponent and to his caddy. Golf has retained much of old time manners and Bobby Jones will be remembered by the older generation for being a gentleman as well as the amateur golfer who led the world.

The 1981 Grand National was won by ALDANITI and second to it, SPARTAN MISSILE, was ridden by John Thorne, who was one of the oldest men ever to ride in the race. What is less known is that SPARTAN MISSILE hit the first fence and I understand hung over it on its tummy. It must have lost lengths trying to get off the fence and back into the race. Yet it was second and although its jockey knew this, he gave both the winner of the race and its jockey Bob Champion, whose life had almost been given up because of cancer, unstinted praise. He never mentioned the fact that his horse may only have lost the race because of what happened at fence one. Great sportsmanship between two of the world's greatest jump jockeys.

Another player, Bjorn Borg, has never shown temper on the tennis court. The saying courtesy costs nothing is perhaps an understatement. Courtesy pays dividends and maybe there is more to the above examples than meets the eye. I believe those who could be described as natural gentlemen, have more composed minds and so are able to devote more energy to winning. We have had too many examples of temper and fighting on tennis courts and playing fields which harm those involved.

DESPERATE NEED FOR SPORTSMANSHIP

No one has researched so far as I know on whether arguing at length with the referee harms him as much as it harms the player. This childish attitude must affect the quality of play. It is worth just a thought how impossible life would be if everyone behaved so badly. Unless in exceptional circumstances such people should be treated with contempt. There may be the occasional need for anger but just as wise business men realise that 90 times out of 100 the customer is right, so in sport it is as important for the players to be fair to the referee, maybe more so.

Sadly, much has changed since if it wasn't "cricket" it wasn't "done", and we in Britain are now among the worst behaved spectators of the Western countries. In many lands one finds less litter lying about. While hooliganism is not confined to Britain we seem to get more of it than some countries but some parts of America are noted for trouble. It is said in Chicago that bullets are the most prevalent cause of death in pregnant women.

I stress these matters because when we discuss them with others it behoves us all to argue for a return to decency and sportsmanship; otherwise things will get worse and end by destroying the way of life, which even still, is unique to our island home.

DO-GOODERS CAN DO HARM

I believe much of our current social malaise results from the exaggerated effect of so many educational do-gooders who took the view that everything was somebody else's fault and that hooliganism was the result of being too strictly brought up. The opposite has transpired and the increase in hooliganism, muggings, etc. seems to grow with reduction in discipline and increasing wealth.

Our comparison is only during living memory and not with two hundred years ago when highway robbery was common and it was not safe to walk at night in London; except for nurses, strangely enough. Since the beginning of this century and until a few years ago people could go anywhere day or night without fear of being attacked, or threatened. This age of returned terror will no doubt be stamped out. We can hope the day will come nearer if all of us try to prevent it especially in teaching children. No one is asking children to be taught to respect merely age but they should be taught to respect decency, fair play, sportsmanship and kindness.

THE DICTATORS OF THE BOX

Television *today* is probably the greatest corruptor of all time. This accrues from the excessive showing of violence, adultery, fornication and drunkenness frequently depicted as jolly everyday happenings. In numerous programmes if the actors are not killing they are in and out of bed or have a bottle of liquor beside them. Could it all be a subtle process of brainwashing passing for entertainment? Near monopoly television has replaced the newspaper as Mr. and Mrs. Average's university.

To be fair a few years ago actors were seen chain-smoking and possibly more than half of them had a cigarette. Not now. The authorities have almost eliminated cigarettes from the box and the middle class public have mostly become non-smokers. Television has led the field in reducing lung cancer; but *it* is a subject with which the authorities seem almost obsessed.

It can be hoped that the scarcity of plays showing the tragedies which result from promiscuity and alcoholism is due only to thoughtlessness for others (etiquette is the opposite) and ignorance of the end results. (See also Chapter 20.)

Britain did not always have such evil or stupid men running television (we didn't need Mary Whitehouses thirty years ago). Let's pray things will improve.

They could hardly get worse. No one wants government censorship but we have a right to expect decency and thoughtfulness from this *near monopoly*. Of course there are many exceptionally fine and interesting programmes but there cannot be any good in the portrayal of so many one-sided and mis-leading films.

23
ETIQUETTE FOR CHILDREN AND BABY SITTERS

Parents should guide their infants in manners so they will not feel too lost when they start school. Children are taught to address their teacher as Sir or Miss or Mrs. X. A few people today imagine that even infants should speak to adults by first names but if children become too familiar with their elders they may be harder to control.

Britain was once famous for its well-mannered children but in some parts of Europe children are better behaved than in modern Britain, where good manners are often cast aside. On a beach in England the uncontrolled shrieking of children can be such as to ruin the holiday for others. This rowdiness and lack of discipline has increased and it is easy to observe it being reflected among the children as they get older and have to face the inevitable disciplines of life. No one wants to be a spoilsport but some restoration of discipline would make children realise what good manners are and how they contribute to happier living.

We are getting a bad name for the appalling manners of our children and perhaps we are receiving our just reward in the extension and increase in rebellious behaviour and hooliganism in our teenagers and young adults. The theory of children being seen and not heard was repressive but the new view that youngsters should be indulged in wherever possible ought not to extend to giving in to them all the time.

It's all a part of the modern teaching of the European so-called progressives who preach that permissiveness in all things leads to a better world. Look around you! So subtle is this false teaching that millions of decent parents have been brainwashed into thinking themselves guilty, and into forgetting that children and the young, although they seem more grown up and sophisticated as a result of watching television, are underneath that veneer, not much different from what they have always been – that is, they need help in growing up if they are to be worthwhile adults, and not spoilt brats.

People who practise good manners seem to find pleasure in life unknown to those who don't. Therefore anything we can do can but be to our credit and their blessing.

BABYSITTING ETIQUETTE

The baby-sitter is a modern substitute for a servant or au pair girl. It has its dangers. Sometimes two girls will baby-sit for the price of one and this is probably a safeguard. The two give some protection against the risk of an intruder or burglar.

Baby-sitters should behave with decorum – neither drinking the householder's sherry nor leaving the place in a mess – and should be mature enough to realise the privilege of being asked to look after a child. Parents should only employ reliable people.

Children under 16 are under the legal age for this responsibility which raises difficulties for both sets of parents. In theory no one of 15 or less ought to be left in charge of infants but in practice, depending on circumstances, exceptions are often made, which is running a risk.

SETTING YOUR CHILDREN AN EXAMPLE

Years ago while criticising one of my children about his swearing he remarked "look who mothered me". This shook me!

No one wants to be a prude but even we adults pick up words from the box. Although well-mannered people won't use them, we hear appalling language so frequently that perhaps most of us, unless we are saints, get a habit of using unnecessary words when angry.

Children should be taught to use discretion in their choice of what to watch on T.V. Fortunately if one picks and chooses there are some excellent programmes.

TEENAGERS

As children develop into the teens their bodies and minds change. For some it is difficult and the parent-child relationship may be disturbed. Children generally worship their parents regarding them as semi-gods but with the teens independence calls and most children naturally begin to want to break away from mum and dad, and take more charge of their own lives.

While young people, because of their years, still lack the experience, which their parents, because of their years, still think they monopolise, to deal with their problems, both parents and children are well advised to remember the iron rule of consideration for others. It sharpens the ability to see that frequently the answer to difficulties is discussion and caring co-operation.

In an ideal relationship both sides should reach happy conclusions, sometimes meeting each other's views part of the way. Unfortunately, the world can be evil and parents may have to make rules about the times children come home or the company they keep, etc. otherwise arguments could be interminable. The young should appreciate this is usually done with good intentions but it is equally up to the parent to try and explain the reasons why actions are taken. Take a child of, say, fifteen, It is only six years since it was nine, whereas a parent of, say, thirty-five has twenty-six years' experience. Make allowance here because there are children who are wiser than their years, just as others develop late.

The teens are a period when it is easy for quarrels to become permanent alienation and both sides should have a mental reservation to avoid temporary bitterness going to extremes. It may be necessary for a parent to show strength by abandoning an argument and going out to dig the garden, or for a child to show strength and go to another room. A frequent parental mistake is to expect their children to do well at school. Perhaps they forget that people like Winston Churchill didn't and neither have many others who reached the top in their own fields. A weakness in judging the young is that the best often develop last. Nor should parents expect their children to be like themselves, just as many youngsters try to be like dad or mum. We should be ourselves.

24
WORD ETIQUETTE

Until some years ago it was customary to call anyone over 25, Mr., Mrs. or Miss.

A change, probably for the better, has taken place and Christian names are the order. This custom blew in over the Atlantic because by the 30s the Americans were calling each other by first names. The head of a business employing 500 people would be called Joe by his floor sweeper, clerk or secretary. Pendulums sometimes swing too far and possibly the Americans are now in reverse on this point whereas here we are into first names almost from the moment of introduction – but not quite. So one has to use discretion. Excessive pride and dignity are useless but sometimes older people *feel* they ought to be respected and one needs to show consideration.

Clergymen, doctors, bankers, solicitors and so on, depend a lot for their livings on dignity, appearances, etc. and few doctors would like you to say " hello doc." Advantages of forename use could be that it may help to reduce class distinction and it could make the world a better place as it is difficult to be nasty or dishonourable with someone you call by their Christian name.

SWEARING

There are few swear words we have not all heard; the captain of a ship is said to have a superior vocabulary and so on but in decent society extreme cursing is avoided. If you hit your thumb with a hammer, you are apt to repeat a word which might begin with "D" or "B". If your penchant is for one beginning with "F" try harder, with the biblical equivalent – "Go forth and multiply!" which helps contracept your language! We have also heard the story of the little girl who asked her mother how the gentleman knew the orange skin he had slipped upon was a blood-orange. So in general don't swear in public although what you say when you cut your lip shaving or when laddering your tights may be different.

TALKING TO YOUR DOCTOR

If you are ill, don't say to the doctor "My abdomen is painful" rather "I have a sore tummy" (or stomach). It is all right to talk to the doctor about your belly for that is how they speak among themselves, although to a layman it sounds crude. To a doctor one can talk of piles or haemorrhoids; similarly it's well-bred to explain that your back passage is itching, or if you prefer rectum. Again anus describes the outer part of the passage which alas can also give trouble but at the moment, the other word beginning with the same letter is unacceptable. (See also chapter 19.)

Friends visiting should be asked (or they may need to ask you) if they want to go to the bathroom, lavatory, even W.C. or smallest room, never in polite company the bog and preferably not toilet which is an Americanism (now replaced by "John"). The jet set would call for the loo but jet people don't always show good taste.

NAUGHTY STORIES

Men tell naughty stories and sometimes they are crude but in good company the filthy story is avoided. Most people enjoy a subtle or reasonable story for a laugh. Britain is the home of such stories. Many countries don't find anything funny in our sexy jokes because often they depend on our colourful variable use of language to which they have no equivalent.

It's no use being too good. *People* are human. Enjoyment should be a big element in our lives. Without relaxation we would all go mad. The warning is avoid too crude stories, expecially in mixed company, and take care how far you go particularly if you are telling a story with a double meaning or inuendo. One should perhaps not go beyond the story of the lady standing beside the headmistress of the school who remarked to her "Isn't that boy in the red trunks a wonderful swimmer?" to which the headmistress replied "and so he ought to be, his mother was a streetwalker in Venice".

Just as people who visit you and drink two-thirds of a bottle of whisky tend to lose invitations, the same applies to people whose stories are crude and unacceptable. It is also wise only to include a story at a time which fits in well with the conversation, otherwise funny or other stories can be a bore.

25
COURTESY OUT OF DOORS

In the old days before we had sex equality, it was customary for a man to walk on the outside of a lady; he was thus nearest the passing traffic and at least in theory he was in a better position to defend his companion if they were attacked by robbers. Things have gone full circle and although now this courtesy has less meaning, with muggers around the habit could do worse than return! If walking with a lady and you walk next to the roadside, she will at any rate know that you have been taught etiquette! It may also prevent her being splashed by traffic.

Where there are no pavements pedestrians should normally try to face any approaching traffic, i.e. in Britain walking on the right hand side of the road viewed towards your destination.

HATS OFF OR SALUTE BUT LADIES FIRST

When meeting a lady it was customary to lift or doff the hat for a moment but with so few men now wearing them this old world acknowledgement is apt to be forgotten. It is still the rule and a sign of good manners. Where no hat is worn the man ought to salute, only not in too military fashion. Alternately, he can smile and bow. This is only a sign of respect to those thought of as the weaker sex. It should be understood that it is the woman's privilege and place to acknowledge the man *first*, either by a smile, nod or wave. If she does not and so "cuts" him, it may imply she does not wish to know him.

Even today among the aristocracy a man wearing a hat will lift it briefly when meeting another gentleman. One would not do this in a football crowd but it is done at fêtes or in "members" areas, at race meetings or at point-to-points and the like.

The common herd, excuse the expression, does not need the manners of kings. Nevertheless knowledge of these rules can be useful. For example in the 1980s in the Royal Enclosure at Ascot one invariably sees men lifting their toppers to other groups of either sex whom they wish to acknowledge.

STAND UP FOR THE OLD AND THE OLD CUSTOMS TOO

While a generation back one would never have seen an old lady standing in a bus or tube, nowadays very few bother to offer a seat. Men and women share the rigours of commuting more equally. Nice people, however, while they would not relinquish their seat to a hockey playing girl, will still offer it to a pregnant woman or disabled person. One must even be careful in showing respect for age, disability or sex – so strong has become the equality kick – some recipients of your goodwill may imagine themselves offended! In the best circles men still open carriage (car) doors and let the ladies enter lifts or go through doors first, but, being gentlemen, do it unobtrusively.

The old aristocracy often personified good taste. Wealth may have had a little to do with it but there was more to it. Workers on the farms and estates as well as domestic servants often became family friends. In many instances such people although knowing what was called "their place" were in some ways like members of the family. The "gentry", as they called their employers, often had cottages reserved into which these old servants and retainers moved on retirement. *Each held the other in respect.* Even today I know several farmers who have built homes for their retired workers.

In those far away days class hate as we know it today was absent. Sadly most of these old families have been wiped out by taxation and frequently replaced by the nouveau riche, many of whom have little of the high-mindedness, devotion to duty and integrity for which Britain was renowned.

The new rich – and the *proportion* of wealthy people in relative terms has not changed – have abandoned many of our old and finest traditions. We are *all* better off now – *except in the timeless and unchanging things that matter.*

Whatever any of us can do by example or by kindness to restore courtesy and decency and art in living happily – while allowing for the changes in detail which have occurred – cannot be bad for the future of our still great country.

INDEX

OUR PUBLISHING POLICY

HOW WE CHOOSE

Our policy is to consider every deserving manuscript and we can give special editorial help where an author is an authority on his subject but an inexperienced writer. We are rigorously selective in the choice of books we publish. We set the highest standards of editorial quality and accuracy. This means that a *Paperfront* is easy to understand and delightful to read. Where illustrations are necessary to convey points of detail, these are drawn up by a subject specialist artist from our panel.

HOW WE KEEP PRICES LOW

We aim for the big seller. This enables us to order enormous print runs and achieve the lowest price for you. Unfortunately, this means that you will not find in the *Paperfront* list any titles on obscure subjects of minority interest only. These could not be printed in large enough quantities to be sold for the low price at which we offer this series.

We sell almost all our *Paperfronts* at the same unit price. This saves a lot of fiddling about in our clerical departments and helps us to give you world-beating value. Under this system, the longer titles are offered at a price which we believe to be unmatched by any publisher in the world.

OUR DISTRIBUTION SYSTEM

Because of the competitive price, and the rapid turnover, *Paperfronts* are possibly the most profitable line a bookseller can handle. They are stocked by the best bookshops all over the world. It may be that your bookseller has run out of stock of a particular title. If so, he can order more from us at any time—we have a fine reputation for "same day" despatch, and we supply any order, however small (even a single copy), to any bookseller who has an account with us. We prefer you to buy from your bookseller, as this reminds him of the strong underlying public demand for *Paperfronts*. Members of the public who live in remote places, or who are housebound, or whose local bookseller is unco-operative, can order direct from us by post.

FREE

If you would like an up-to-date list of all the paperfront titles currently available, send a stamped self-addressed envelope to
ELLIOT RIGHT WAY BOOKS, BRIGHTON RD.,
LOWER KINGSWOOD, SURREY, U.K.